The Data Center: The Engine Behind Artificial Intelligence

By Susie Hala

AI Educator | Author | Founder of the IntelliGloss Educational Series

An IntelliGloss AI Education Series Book

Published by IntelliGloss Press

United States of America

Legal Disclaimer

Educational Purpose Disclaimer

"This publication is part of the IntelliGloss AI Education Series, a structured curriculum support system for AI literacy in grades 6–12."

The information presented in this publication is provided for educational and informational purposes only. This book is intended to support educators, administrators, parents, and learners in understanding the concepts, opportunities, and challenges associated with artificial intelligence in education. It is not intended to serve as legal, technical, policy, cybersecurity, or professional advice.

Readers should consult qualified professionals, institutional guidelines, and local regulations before implementing any educational programs, technologies, or policies described in this book.

Technology and Accuracy Disclaimer
Artificial intelligence is a rapidly evolving field. While every effort has been made to ensure the accuracy and reliability of the information presented at the time of publication, technologies, policies, research findings, and best practices may change over time. The author and publisher make no guarantees that all information will remain current or applicable in future technological environments.

Readers are encouraged to verify tools, platforms, and recommendations independently before using them in educational settings.

Implementation Responsibility
Schools, educators, and institutions are solely responsible for determining how and whether to implement artificial intelligence tools, strategies, or classroom activities discussed in this book. Educational environments vary widely, and policies regarding technology use, student privacy, and curriculum development differ by district, state, and country.

The author and publisher assume no responsibility for outcomes resulting from the implementation of ideas, examples, or frameworks described in this book.

Student Safety and Data Privacy
Artificial intelligence tools may involve the collection or processing of data. Educators and institutions are responsible for ensuring that any technology used complies with applicable student privacy laws, data protection regulations, and school policies, including but not limited to FERPA, COPPA, GDPR, or other relevant regulations depending on jurisdiction.

The author and publisher are not responsible for the privacy practices, security policies, or data handling procedures of third-party platforms or software mentioned in this book.

Third-Party Tools and References
This book may reference third-party technologies, organizations, research studies, or platforms for illustrative and educational purposes. Such references do not constitute endorsements or guarantees regarding the performance, reliability, safety, or suitability of those tools for educational use.

Educators and institutions should conduct their own evaluations and risk assessments before adopting any technology.

No Professional Liability
The author and publisher shall not be held liable for any direct, indirect, incidental, or consequential damages resulting from the use or misuse of the information contained in this book. This includes but is not limited to decisions related to curriculum design, technology adoption, classroom instruction, institutional policies, or educational outcomes.

Educational Interpretation
The concepts and examples provided in this book are intended to support discussion and learning. They should not be interpreted as official standards, mandatory guidelines, or universally applicable policies for artificial intelligence education.

Schools and educators are encouraged to adapt the ideas presented here according to their local policies, cultural context, educational standards, and student needs.

Author's Intent
The goal of this book is to promote responsible AI literacy, thoughtful discussion, and ethical awareness as schools prepare students for a world increasingly shaped by intelligent technologies.

The author encourages readers to approach artificial intelligence education with curiosity, caution, and a commitment to responsible learning.

Title: The Data Center: The Engine Behind Artificial Intelligence

ISBN: 9781972925058

Published by
IntelliGloss Press
United States of America

Dedication

This book is dedicated to the next generation of learners—
the students who will grow up in a world shaped by intelligent technology,
and who deserve to understand it with clarity, confidence, and purpose.

To the educators who show up every day with dedication and heart,
guiding students through a rapidly changing world—
your role has never been more important.

To the parents and families who support learning at home,
encouraging curiosity, responsibility, and growth—
you are the foundation of every child's success.

And to my granddaughters,
whose curiosity, imagination, and future inspire me to do this work—
this book is for you.

May you not only learn how to use technology,
but understand it, question it, and shape it for the good of others.

About the Author

Susie Hala
Founder of the IntelliGloss AI Education Series

Susie Hala is an author, educator, and curriculum developer dedicated to advancing artificial intelligence literacy in education. Her work focuses on helping schools, educators, and students understand how intelligent technologies are shaping modern society—and why that understanding is essential for the next generation.

Hala is the creator of the IntelliGloss AI Education Series, a comprehensive and growing collection of educational books designed to make complex artificial intelligence concepts accessible, structured, and practical for classroom use. Her work emphasizes clarity, organization, and responsible implementation, enabling schools to introduce AI literacy without requiring advanced technical backgrounds.

In addition to her work in education, Hala brings hands-on experience working with artificial intelligence systems, including early exposure to rule-based AI technologies during her time working with AT&T. She has also developed modern digital platforms that integrate artificial intelligence, automation, and online systems, building e-commerce solutions and AI-driven applications that connect payment platforms, hosting environments, and conversational AI tools into real-world, functional systems.

This combination of foundational understanding and practical experience allows her to translate complex AI concepts into clear, accessible language for both educators and students.

Recognizing that artificial intelligence is rapidly transforming how information is created, interpreted, and used, Hala advocates for equipping students with the ability not only to use AI tools, but to understand, question, and evaluate them. Her work emphasizes critical thinking, ethical awareness, and responsible digital citizenship.

The IntelliGloss AI Education Series supports schools in teaching key areas such as artificial intelligence foundations, algorithms, machine learning concepts, and AI ethics, as well as the broader evolution of intelligent systems—from Artificial Narrow Intelligence (ANI) to Artificial General Intelligence (AGI) and Artificial Superintelligence (ASI). These resources are designed for students in grades 6–12 and for educators seeking structured, classroom-ready approaches to AI literacy.

In addition to her work in education publishing, Hala has a strong background in entrepreneurship, having built and managed multiple businesses and educational initiatives. Her experience across industries reinforces her belief that technology education must remain grounded in human values, critical thinking, and ethical responsibility.

Her mission is clear: to ensure that the next generation understands intelligent technology—not just how to use it, but how it truly works.

Preface

Two Students. Two Paths. One Future.

Before we begin, it is important to understand why learning how artificial intelligence works—not just how to use it—matters for every student.

Imagine two students who have just graduated from high school and are preparing for a job interview. The first student knows how to use artificial intelligence tools. This student can generate answers, complete assignments quickly, and rely on AI to assist with tasks. However, this student does not understand how artificial intelligence works behind the scenes.

The second student also knows how to use AI tools, but in addition, understands the foundational concepts behind them. This student has learned about data, algorithms, tokens, models, and how intelligent systems are trained and operate. This student can think critically about AI, recognize its limitations, and adapt when needed.

At first, the first student may appear faster and more efficient. However, over time, the second student demonstrates a deeper level of understanding, independence, and problem-solving ability. The second student is not only able to use artificial intelligence but also to question it, improve it, and grow with it.

This book is written for the second student.

In a world where artificial intelligence is becoming part of everyday life, students must not only learn how to use intelligent systems—they must learn how they work. True understanding leads to confidence, responsibility, and the ability to lead in an AI-driven future.

This perspective is not just theoretical—it is personal.

There was a time when I was the first student.

I knew how to use systems. I followed processes, completed tasks, and worked within structured environments that required accuracy and consistency. At the time, I did not think of these systems as artificial intelligence. They were simply part of the job—tools that had to be learned, followed, and mastered.

But looking back, I now understand something much deeper. I was working within rule-based systems—the earliest foundation of what we now recognize as artificial intelligence.

That realization changed everything.

As I began studying modern AI, including machine learning, deep learning, and intelligent systems, I started to see a clear connection between the past and the present. The structured systems I once worked in, the logic behind decision-making, and the step-by-step processes all still exist today. They have simply evolved.

Artificial intelligence did not appear overnight. It grew from rule-based systems into systems that can now learn, adapt, and assist in ways we never imagined.

I made a decision to move from simply using systems to understanding them.

That journey—from student one to student two—is the reason these books exist.

My mission is to help others bridge that same gap.

I believe that artificial intelligence should be understandable for everyone. It should not feel intimidating or out of reach. Students should feel confident exploring it. Teachers should feel prepared to introduce it. Everyday learners should have access to clear, structured explanations that make sense.

You do not need a background in technology. You do not need to know how to code. You only need the right explanation.

A Note from the Author

AI Is a Tool — Not a Decision Maker

Artificial Intelligence is becoming part of everyday life. Students use it to complete assignments, teachers use it to support instruction, and businesses use it to improve efficiency. While these tools are powerful and useful, there is an important truth that must remain clear from the very beginning:

Artificial Intelligence does not make decisions—people do.

One of the main purposes of this book is to help readers understand how AI works, what it can do, and—just as importantly—what it cannot do. AI systems are designed to process information, identify patterns, and generate responses based on data. They can assist with thinking, but they do not think independently. They can provide answers, but they do not understand consequences. They can suggest ideas, but they do not choose actions.

Every outcome that involves AI begins and ends with human involvement. A person asks the question. A person reviews the response. A person decides what to do next. Responsibility does not transfer to the machine.

In today's world, it is easy to confuse speed with intelligence and automation with authority. Because AI can respond quickly and confidently, it may appear as though it is making decisions. In reality, it is performing a task based on patterns it has learned—not exercising judgment.

This distinction matters. When people begin to rely on AI without understanding its role, they risk misunderstanding information, misusing technology, or placing trust in a system that is not capable of accountability. Clear understanding leads to responsible use.

This book was written to remove confusion and provide clarity. It is designed to help students and educators move beyond simply using AI tools and begin understanding the structure behind them. By learning how AI supports human thinking—rather than replacing it—readers can approach technology with confidence, awareness, and responsibility.

Artificial Intelligence is a powerful assistant. It can enhance learning, support creativity, and improve productivity. But it remains a tool.

The decisions, the actions, and the responsibility will always belong to the human.

— Susie Hala

Bringing Clarity to Artificial Intelligence

During a recent meeting with a school district, it became clear that one of the biggest challenges in artificial intelligence education is not the technology itself—but the way it is explained.

In that discussion, terms such as **chatbots, generative AI, agentic AI, autonomy, tools, hallucinations, and AI usage levels** were all mentioned together. While each term represents a distinct concept, they were often blended into one conversation without clear distinctions. The result was confusion, even among those who were actively trying to understand and make informed decisions.

This experience revealed an important truth:
Without clear definitions and structure, artificial intelligence becomes difficult to teach, difficult to learn, and difficult to use responsibly.

This book is designed to provide that structure.

Understanding the Core Concepts

To build a strong foundation, it is essential to separate and define the key ideas that are often confused.

Chatbot
A chatbot is a conversational interface that allows users to interact with an AI system through questions and prompts. It responds to input but does not act beyond what is directly requested.

Generative AI (Gen AI)
Generative AI refers to systems that create new content, including text, images, audio, and code. These systems generate outputs based on patterns learned from large datasets. While powerful, generative AI does not truly understand information and may occasionally produce inaccurate results.

Agentic AI
Agentic AI describes systems that can take action toward a goal. Rather than responding to a single prompt, these systems can plan, make decisions within defined limits, and carry out multi-step tasks. This introduces a higher level of functional independence.

Autonomy
Autonomy refers to how independently an AI system operates. Some systems require constant human guidance, while others can perform multiple steps with minimal input. Autonomy is not a separate type of AI, but a measure of how much control the system has in completing tasks.

Additional Terms That Shape Understanding

AI Tools
AI tools are the applications people use to interact with artificial intelligence, such as writing assistants, design platforms, and data analysis systems. These tools make AI accessible in everyday tasks.

Hallucination
A hallucination occurs when an AI system generates information that appears correct but is inaccurate or unsupported. This is a known limitation of generative systems and highlights the need for human verification.

The AI Use Continuum

Another important concept is how AI is used at different levels. Rather than viewing AI as a single capability, it is more accurate to understand it as a continuum of use:

Assistive Use
AI supports simple tasks such as answering questions, correcting grammar, or providing suggestions.

Augmented Use
AI helps expand human capability by generating ideas, organizing content, and assisting in problem-solving.

Agentic Use
AI begins to take on multi-step responsibilities, planning and completing tasks with reduced human input.

This continuum shows that AI can range from a helpful assistant to a more independent system, depending on how it is applied.

The Moment Everything Sounded Like One Conversation

During a recent discussion on artificial intelligence, I listened closely as different experts spoke about the future of AI. One referenced advanced systems beyond human intelligence, another discussed goal-driven AI systems, and the conversation shifted quickly between topics like autonomy, tools, and system behavior. At first, it sounded like a single, unified discussion. But the more I listened, the more I realized something important.

They were not all talking about the same thing.

One part of the conversation focused on future possibilities—high-level systems that do not yet exist. Another part focused on current technologies that are already being used today. At the same time, different terms were being used to describe how AI behaves, how it makes decisions, and how much independence it may have. These ideas were layered together in a way that made them sound connected, even when they were not.

This experience revealed a major challenge in understanding artificial intelligence today. Many discussions combine different types of AI, different levels of intelligence, and different behaviors into one conversation. Without clear structure, these ideas begin to blur together. For someone trying to learn, this can feel overwhelming and confusing.

This book is built to solve that problem.

Artificial intelligence is not one single concept. It is a system made up of multiple layers. Some layers describe how intelligent a system is. Other layers describe how the system behaves. Still others describe how much control or independence the system has. When these layers are separated and explained clearly, AI becomes much easier to understand.

The goal of this book is to bring clarity where confusion often exists. Instead of mixing everything into one explanation, each concept is presented in a structured and organized way. This allows students, educators, and readers to see how the pieces fit together without losing sight of what each part actually means.

Understanding artificial intelligence begins with understanding its structure.

Once that structure is clear, the conversation becomes clearer as well.

Why Clarity Matters

When these concepts are not clearly defined, they merge into what can be described as a "conceptual blur." This can lead to misunderstandings about what AI can and cannot do, as well as unrealistic expectations or misuse in educational settings.

Clear understanding helps ensure that:

Students remain active learners, not passive users

Educators maintain control over instructional outcomes

AI is used as a support tool rather than a replacement for thinking

The Purpose of This Book

This book is built on a simple but essential principle:

Students should not only use artificial intelligence—they should understand it.

By clearly defining core concepts such as chatbots, generative AI, agentic AI, autonomy, and the continuum of AI use, this curriculum provides a structured pathway for developing both technical understanding and critical thinking.

Artificial intelligence is not a single tool or system. It is a collection of capabilities that must be understood in context.

Clarity is the foundation of responsible innovation.

Structuring Artificial Intelligence to Create Clarity and Understanding

Why Structure Is Necessary

Artificial intelligence is often presented as one unified concept. In many discussions, different ideas such as intelligence level, system behavior, and autonomy are combined into a single explanation. This can make AI appear more complex and confusing than it actually is.

Clarity begins when these ideas are separated and organized.

Structuring artificial intelligence allows each concept to be understood on its own before being connected to the larger system.

The Problem Without Structure

When AI is not structured, conversations may include multiple terms that sound related but describe entirely different things. For example, a discussion may move quickly between advanced future systems, current tools, and system behaviors without clearly distinguishing between them.

This creates the impression that all forms of AI operate at the same level and in the same way, which is not accurate.

Without structure, understanding becomes difficult.

The Solution: A Structured Approach

Artificial intelligence becomes clearer when it is organized into distinct categories.

Level explains how intelligent a system is.
Behavior explains how the system operates.
Control explains how much independence the system has.

Each category answers a different question. Together, they form a complete picture of how AI systems function.

Clarity Through Separation

A system can operate at a current level of intelligence while demonstrating different behaviors or levels of independence. For example, a system that generates responses and a system that takes steps toward completing a task may operate at the same intelligence level but differ in how they behave.

This distinction becomes clear only when structure is applied.

Instructional Insight

When teaching artificial intelligence, it is important to avoid presenting all concepts at once. Separating ideas into categories allows learners to focus on one dimension at a time, building understanding step by step.

Structured learning leads to deeper comprehension.

Key Takeaway

Artificial intelligence is not one single idea. It is a system made up of multiple parts. Structuring those parts creates clarity, improves understanding, and allows learners to see how the system truly works.

Reflection Question

How does separating intelligence level, behavior, and control make artificial intelligence easier to understand?

The IntelliGloss Instructional Approach

The IntelliGloss AI Education Series is designed to help students move beyond simply using AI tools and begin understanding artificial intelligence as a complete system.

Students learn how AI is built, how it operates, and how it connects to the real world.

A Message to Students and Readers

If you have ever felt that technology was too complicated…
If you have ever been confused by systems that were never clearly explained…

I want you to know:

You are capable of understanding artificial intelligence.

Sometimes, the challenge is not the concept itself—it is how it has been presented.

This series was created to change that.

A Message to Educators

To the educators using this material:

These books are designed to support you in introducing artificial intelligence in a way that is clear, structured, and meaningful for students.

AI is becoming part of every industry, and students deserve more than just exposure to tools—they deserve understanding.

This series aims to provide that foundation.

Final Reflection

Every experience we have—especially the challenging ones—prepares us for something greater.

The systems I once worked in taught me discipline, structure, and attention to detail. Today, those same lessons allow me to break down complex ideas and make them understandable for others.

That is what this series represents:

Turning complexity into clarity.

Why Artificial Intelligence Education Matters for Every Student

Why AI Literacy Is Essential for Every Student

Artificial intelligence is no longer a future concept or a specialized technology used only by experts. It is already part of everyday life for students of all ages. From smartphones and search engines to navigation apps, social media, streaming platforms, and educational tools, AI systems influence how information is accessed, decisions are made, and learning takes place.

Because AI is embedded in daily life, understanding it is no longer optional. It is a foundational skill, similar to digital literacy and critical thinking. Students do not need to become programmers or engineers, but they do need to understand what AI is, how it works at a basic level, and how it affects their lives.

AI education should not be limited to computer science classrooms. Every student interacts with AI systems daily. Teaching students how these systems function empowers them to become informed users rather than passive consumers of technology.

This book is designed to make artificial intelligence understandable, approachable, and relevant. It focuses on clarity, responsibility, and real-world understanding to help students prepare for a future where humans and intelligent systems work side by side.

IntelliGloss AI Education Series

Teaching how AI actually works—from hardware to power to global systems.

Why AI Education Matters

Artificial intelligence is already shaping how students learn, write, research, and solve problems.

Yet many students—and educators—are using AI tools without understanding how these systems actually work.

Schools need more than access to technology.
They need structured, responsible AI education.

Our Approach

The IntelliGloss AI Education Series is designed to help students move beyond simply using AI tools and begin understanding artificial intelligence as a complete system.

Students learn how AI is built, how it operates, and how it connects to the real world.

The IntelliGloss Framework

Our books introduce AI through a clear and connected system:

- **Chip Family** — the hardware that powers AI
- **Watts Family** — the rate at which AI uses power
- **Energy Family** — the total power AI consumes over time
- **Infrastructure Family** — the global systems that support AI

This framework helps students understand AI from the inside out.

Built for the Classroom

Each book includes:

- Structured chapters aligned with semester learning
- Clear explanations designed for student understanding
- Reflection sections with learning objectives
- Worksheets, quizzes, and answer keys
- Teacher Implementation Guides

Supporting Schools and Educators

The IntelliGloss series supports:

- Responsible and ethical AI use
- Student data awareness and safety
- Critical thinking and digital literacy
- Classroom-ready instruction for grades 6–12 and beyond

What This Book Is—and What It Is Not

Many people today are becoming familiar with artificial intelligence through tools like ChatGPT, Microsoft Copilot, Canva, and other AI-powered applications. These tools can help with writing, answering questions, creating images, and completing everyday tasks.

In addition to these tools, you may also hear terms such as **AI agents, agentic AI, autonomous systems, and generative AI**. While these may sound complex, they are all part of the same evolving landscape of artificial intelligence technologies.

This book is not a guide on how to use those tools.

Instead, it explains what makes those tools possible.

Behind every AI tool is a system made up of multiple layers working together. At the most basic level, information is represented as bits and processed through powerful computer chips. That information is organized into data, broken into tokens, and then processed by algorithms and models that allow the system to recognize patterns, generate responses, and perform tasks.

These components—chips, bits, tokens, data, algorithms, and models—work together as a complete system. While users may only see the tool, the real intelligence comes from how these underlying parts interact behind the scenes.

Artificial intelligence can also be understood in terms of different levels of capability. Most of the AI systems used today fall under **Artificial Narrow Intelligence (ANI)**, which is designed to perform specific tasks, such as answering questions or generating content. More advanced forms, such as **Artificial General Intelligence (AGI)** and **Artificial Superintelligence (ASI)** represent future possibilities where AI could match or exceed human-level thinking. While these advanced levels are still theoretical, understanding the differences helps provide a broader view of where AI is today and where it may be heading.

For students, parents, and educators, this distinction is important. Learning how to use AI tools is helpful, but understanding how they work—and where they fit within the larger AI landscape—builds stronger thinking, better decision-making, and more responsible use.

Most importantly, artificial intelligence does not make decisions on its own. It does not take responsibility for actions or outcomes. AI systems generate responses based on data and patterns, but it is always the human who decides what to do with that information.

This book is designed to make these underlying systems clear and accessible, even for readers who are new to artificial intelligence.

Artificial intelligence is still in its early stages of development. As these technologies continue to grow, those who understand the foundation behind them will be better prepared to adapt, question, and use them wisely.

Who This Book Is For

This book is designed for educators, school leaders, and curriculum developers guiding students in an age of rapidly advancing technology.

Artificial intelligence is already influencing how students learn, research, and communicate. Yet many educators have not received formal training in how these systems work or how they should be addressed in the classroom.

This book helps bridge that gap by providing clear explanations and practical frameworks for understanding artificial intelligence in an educational setting.

How Schools Can Use This Book

This book supports schools in developing a structured approach to artificial intelligence literacy.

It can be used for:

Professional development for educators

Classroom discussions and activities

Curriculum support across subject areas

Policy and academic integrity conversations

Rather than focusing on specific tools, this book emphasizes lasting principles that help students understand, evaluate, and use AI responsibly.

Closing Perspective

Artificial intelligence will continue to evolve. With the right knowledge and leadership, schools can ensure that students not only use these technologies, but understand them, question them, and apply them responsibly.

IntelliGloss is more than a book series. It is a structured approach to preparing students for a future shaped by artificial intelligence.

Rather than focusing only on how to use AI tools, this series helps students understand how AI actually works—from its foundational building blocks to real-world applications.

"Before exploring the technical structure of artificial intelligence, it is equally important to understand the human principles that guide its use."

Human Values Family

Definition

The Human Values Family in artificial intelligence represents the guiding principles that shape how AI systems are created, used, and integrated into society. These values include ethics, responsibility, trust, and human well-being.

Artificial intelligence may be built on data, algorithms, and computational systems, but its true impact is measured by how it affects people. For this reason, AI is not only a technical system—it is a human-centered system.

Key Concepts

The Human Values Family exists to ensure that artificial intelligence serves humanity in a positive and responsible way. While AI systems can process information and generate outcomes, they do not possess judgment, empathy, or moral understanding.

This means that human values must guide every stage of AI development—from design to deployment.

AI reflects the intentions, decisions, and assumptions of the people who build and use it. If those values are not carefully considered, AI systems can unintentionally produce biased, harmful, or misleading results.

Understanding human values in AI is not optional—it is essential.

Core Elements of the Human Values Family

Ethics
Ethics in AI refers to making decisions that are fair, just, and respectful of human rights. This includes minimizing bias, protecting privacy, and ensuring transparency in how systems operate.

Responsibility
Responsibility means that humans remain accountable for AI systems. Developers, educators, organizations, and users must take ownership of how AI is used and the outcomes it produces.

Trust
Trust is critical for the successful adoption of AI. People must feel confident that AI systems are reliable, safe, and aligned with their best interests.

Human Well-Being
AI should enhance human life—not replace, harm, or diminish it. This includes supporting

learning, improving access to information, and creating opportunities while maintaining human dignity.

Real-World Connection

Artificial intelligence is already influencing how people learn, communicate, and make decisions. From search engines to classroom tools, AI is shaping daily experiences.

Without clear human values guiding these systems, there is a risk of reinforcing misinformation, bias, or unrealistic expectations.

For students, this means learning not only how to use AI tools, but how to question them, evaluate their outputs, and understand their limitations.

Applications in Education

In the classroom, the Human Values Family helps students develop critical thinking and ethical awareness. Teachers can use this framework to guide discussions about fairness, responsibility, and the impact of technology on society.

Students can explore questions such as:

How should AI be used responsibly?

What makes an AI system fair?

How does technology influence human behavior?

This approach supports both technical understanding and responsible decision-making.

Benefits

Teaching human values in AI helps students:

Develop ethical awareness

Strengthen critical thinking

Understand the societal impact of technology

Become responsible users and future creators of AI

It ensures that learning about AI goes beyond functionality and includes responsibility.

Challenges

Human values are not always universal. Different cultures, communities, and individuals may have different perspectives on what is considered fair or ethical.

Additionally, AI technology is evolving rapidly, often faster than policies and guidelines can keep up. This makes it essential for educators and students to stay informed and adaptable.

Summary

The Human Values Family reminds us that artificial intelligence is not just about machines—it is about people.

By focusing on ethics, responsibility, trust, and human well-being, students can learn to use AI thoughtfully and responsibly.

Understanding these principles helps prepare learners to navigate a world where artificial intelligence plays an increasingly important role in everyday life.

Executive Summary

IntelliGloss AI Education Series

Teaching How Artificial Intelligence Actually Works

Artificial intelligence is already shaping how students learn, write, research, and make decisions. Yet in many classrooms, students are being introduced to AI tools without understanding how these systems actually function.

This creates a critical gap.

Students may become efficient users of technology, but without foundational knowledge, they are not equipped to think critically, evaluate outputs, or use AI responsibly. As AI continues to expand across every industry, this gap will only grow more significant.

The **IntelliGloss AI Education Series** was created to address this challenge.

The Problem

Most current approaches to AI in education focus on tool usage rather than system understanding. As a result:

- Students rely on AI without understanding its limitations
- Educators lack structured frameworks for teaching AI concepts
- Key terms such as generative AI, agentic AI, and autonomy are often introduced without clear definitions
- Responsibility and ethical use are not consistently emphasized

Without clarity, artificial intelligence becomes difficult to teach, difficult to learn, and difficult to manage in a school environment.

The Solution

The IntelliGloss AI Education Series provides a structured, classroom-ready approach to artificial intelligence literacy for grades 6–12.

Rather than focusing on individual tools, this series teaches students how AI works as a complete system—from foundational components to real-world applications.

Students learn to move beyond surface-level interaction and develop true understanding.

The IntelliGloss Framework

The series introduces AI through a clear and connected structure, including:

- Foundational building blocks such as data, algorithms, tokens, and models
- System-level understanding through categories such as intelligence level, behavior, and control
- Real-world context through applications, limitations, and responsible use
- Human-centered learning through ethics, responsibility, trust, and student safety

This structured approach transforms artificial intelligence from a confusing concept into an understandable system.

Instructional Design

Each book in the series is designed for practical classroom use and includes:

- Structured chapters aligned with instructional pacing
- Clear, student-friendly explanations
- Reflection sections to reinforce understanding
- Worksheets, quizzes, and answer keys
- Teacher implementation support

No prior technical background is required for educators or students.

Guiding Principle

A central message of the IntelliGloss series is:

Artificial Intelligence is a tool—not a decision maker.

Students learn that while AI can support thinking and provide information, all decisions, actions, and responsibilities remain with humans. This principle reinforces critical thinking, accountability, and responsible technology use.

Why It Matters

AI literacy is no longer optional. It is a foundational skill.

Students who understand how AI works will be better prepared to:

- Think critically about information
- Adapt to emerging technologies
- Use AI responsibly and ethically
- Succeed in an increasingly AI-driven world

Our Goal

The IntelliGloss AI Education Series is designed to help schools move beyond simply using artificial intelligence tools and toward a deeper understanding of how these systems actually work.

By providing clear structure, defined concepts, and real-world context, this series equips students and educators with the knowledge needed to think critically, evaluate information, and use AI responsibly.

The goal is not just to introduce technology—but to build understanding, confidence, and accountability in an AI-driven world.

This is not just about learning to use AI—it is about preparing students to understand it, question it, and lead with it.

Clarity leads to confidence.
Understanding leads to responsible use.

Mission Statement

The mission of the IntelliGloss AI Education Series is to make artificial intelligence clear, structured, and accessible for every student and educator.

In a world where AI is rapidly transforming how information is created, used, and understood, this series is designed to move beyond surface-level interaction and provide a deeper understanding of how intelligent systems actually work.

Through clear explanations, organized frameworks, and real-world context, IntelliGloss equips learners with the ability to think critically, evaluate information, and engage with technology responsibly.

This mission is grounded in a simple belief:
students should not only learn how to use artificial intelligence—they should understand it.

By building both technical awareness and human-centered understanding, the IntelliGloss AI Education Series prepares students to navigate, question, and shape a future increasingly influenced by intelligent technologies.

The goal is not just to keep up with artificial intelligence—but to understand it, guide it, and use it responsibly.

Vision Statement

The vision of the IntelliGloss AI Education Series is to create a future where artificial intelligence is clearly understood, responsibly used, and thoughtfully integrated into education and everyday life.

In this future, students are not passive users of technology, but informed thinkers who understand how intelligent systems work, recognize their limitations, and apply them with purpose and responsibility.

Educators are equipped with clear frameworks and structured resources that make artificial intelligence accessible, teachable, and meaningful across all subjects—not just in technical fields.

Schools become environments where technology is not simply adopted, but understood—where students are encouraged to question, evaluate, and engage with AI in ways that support learning, creativity, and ethical awareness.

As artificial intelligence continues to evolve, this vision supports a generation that is prepared not only to adapt to change, but to lead it with knowledge, confidence, and integrity.

The future of artificial intelligence will not be defined by technology alone—but by the understanding and responsibility of those who use it.

Connecting AI Understanding to Cybersecurity Awareness

Definition

Understanding artificial intelligence is the first step toward understanding cybersecurity. While cybersecurity focuses on protecting systems, data, and users, artificial intelligence explains how those systems are built, how they function, and where they may be vulnerable.

The Connection

Every AI system is made up of components such as data, algorithms, models, and infrastructure. These same components are also the targets of cybersecurity threats.

When students understand:

How data is collected and stored

How algorithms make decisions

How AI models process information

How systems operate across frontend and backend layers

They begin to recognize where risks can exist and how systems can be misused.

Why This Matters

In today's digital world, students are not just users of technology—they are participants in complex systems powered by artificial intelligence.

Without understanding how these systems work:

Technology becomes something they trust without question

Risks become harder to recognize

Decisions are made without awareness of consequences

With understanding:

Students become more aware of how their data is used

They recognize how systems can be manipulated

They make more informed and responsible choices

Building Digital Readiness

Digital readiness is not only about using tools. It is about understanding the systems behind those tools.

By learning how AI works, students develop:

Awareness of digital environments

Confidence in navigating technology

A foundation for future learning, including cybersecurity

Conclusion

Cybersecurity begins with understanding.

Before students can protect systems, they must first understand how those systems are built and how they operate. This is why learning artificial intelligence is not only about innovation—it is also about responsibility.

The Foundation of Artificial Intelligence

Definition

The foundation of Artificial Intelligence (AI) refers to the core building blocks that allow AI systems to function. These building blocks work together to help machines learn from information, recognize patterns, and make decisions. AI is not magic—it is a system built on structured components that operate behind the scenes.

Understanding the Foundation in Simple Terms

Artificial Intelligence can be compared to a house. Before a house is complete, it must be built on a strong foundation. This foundation includes concrete, wiring, plumbing, and support structures that are not always visible but are essential for the house to function properly.

In the same way, AI systems rely on foundational components that are not visible to users but are necessary for AI tools to work. When people use AI applications such as chatbots or design tools, they are interacting with the surface. The true power of AI comes from what is underneath.

Key Components of the AI Foundation

1. Data (The Information)

Data is the starting point of all AI systems. It includes text, images, numbers, audio, and other forms of information. AI systems learn by analyzing patterns within this data.

2. Algorithms (The Instructions)

Algorithms are step-by-step instructions that tell the AI system how to process data. They guide how the system learns, identifies patterns, and produces results.

3. Models (The Trained System)

A model is created when data and algorithms are combined through a training process. The model acts as the "brain" of the AI system, allowing it to make predictions and generate responses.

4. Computing Power (The Engine)

AI systems require powerful computers to process large amounts of data. This includes specialized hardware such as processors and graphics processing units (GPUs) that allow AI to function efficiently.

5. Infrastructure (The Environment)

Infrastructure refers to the systems that support AI operations, including servers, storage, networks, and energy systems. Data centers are a key part of this infrastructure, providing the physical space where AI systems operate.

How These Components Work Together

AI systems function by combining all foundational components into a single process. Data is collected and analyzed using algorithms. This process creates a model that can recognize patterns and make decisions. The entire system is powered by computing machines and supported by infrastructure.

Why Understanding the Foundation Matters

Many people use AI tools without understanding how they work. This can lead to confusion, misuse, or over-reliance on technology. By understanding the foundation of AI, students and educators can:

- Develop critical thinking skills
- Use AI tools more responsibly
- Recognize the limitations of AI systems

Build a deeper understanding of modern technology

Real-World Example

When a student asks a chatbot a question, the response does not come from "thinking" like a human. Instead, the AI system uses a trained model that has learned patterns from large amounts of data. It follows algorithms to predict the most appropriate answer, using powerful computers and infrastructure to deliver the response quickly.

This process is also influenced by how the question is asked. The words, structure, and clarity of a question—often referred to as a *prompt*—can affect the quality of the response. Learning how to communicate effectively with AI systems is an important skill known as prompt engineering. For further understanding, students and educators may explore *What to Say When You Talk to Yourself: A Guide to Prompt Engineering* by Susie Hala, which explains how carefully structured prompts can guide AI responses more effectively.

Conclusion

The foundation of Artificial Intelligence is built on data, algorithms, models, computing power, and infrastructure. These components work together to create systems that can learn, predict, and assist humans. Understanding this foundation helps students move beyond simply using AI tools and toward truly understanding how artificial intelligence works.

The Foundational Families of Artificial Intelligence

Introduction

Artificial intelligence is often described as a powerful technology, but in reality, it is not a single system. It is a combination of multiple components working together to create intelligent behavior.

To better understand how artificial intelligence works, it is helpful to break it down into organized groups. In the IntelliGloss framework, these groups are called **Foundational Families of Artificial Intelligence**.

Each family represents a key part of how AI systems are built and operate. Some families focus on how information is created and stored. Others focus on how machines learn, make decisions, process language, or perform tasks. Additional families represent the physical hardware, energy systems, and global infrastructure that make artificial intelligence possible.

When these families work together, they form a complete AI system.

This approach allows students and educators to move beyond simply using artificial intelligence tools and begin to understand what is happening behind the scenes. Instead of viewing AI as a mystery, learners can see it as a structured system made up of clearly defined components.

The diagram on the next page provides a visual overview of these families and how they connect to form the foundation of artificial intelligence.

By learning each family step by step, students develop a deeper understanding of how AI systems process information, learn from data, and interact with the world.

Understanding the Foundational Families of Artificial Intelligence is the first step toward true AI literacy.

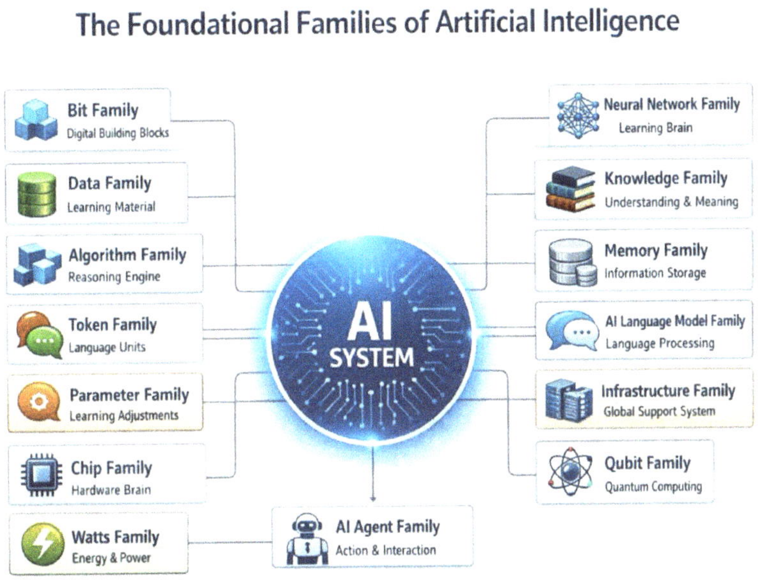

The Foundational Families of Artificial Intelligence

Bit Family
Digital Building Blocks
Data Family
Learning Material
Algorithm Family
Reasoning Engine
Token Family
Language Units
Parameter Family
Learning Adjustments
Chip Family
Hardware Brain
Watts Family
Energy & Power
AI SYSTEM
AI Agent Family
Action & Interaction
Neural Network Family
Learning Brain
Knowledge Family
Understanding & Meaning
Memory Family
Information Storage
AI Language Model Family
Language Processing
Infrastructure Family
Global Support System
Qubit Family
Quantum Computing

The Foundational Families of Artificial Intelligence

Family	Role	Description
Bit Family	Digital Building Blocks	The smallest unit of digital information (0 or 1). All computing systems begin with bits.
Algorithm Family	Reasoning Engine	Step-by-step instructions that tell computers how to solve problems and process information.
Token Family	Language Units	Pieces of text used by AI models to understand and generate human language.

Family	Role	Description
Parameter Family	Learning Adjustment System	Adjustable numerical values inside AI models that allow them to learn patterns from data.
Data Family	Learning Material	The information AI studies in order to learn patterns, relationships, and knowledge.
Logic Family	Decision Rules	The reasoning structures that allow AI systems to make decisions and evaluate conditions.
Memory Family	Information Storage	Systems that store and retrieve information so AI models can access past knowledge and context.
Knowledge Family	Understanding & Meaning	Structured information that allows AI to represent facts, relationships, and concepts.
Neural Network Family	Learning Brain	Interconnected layers of artificial neurons that enable AI systems to recognize patterns, learn from data, and make predictions.
AI Model Family	Intelligence Engine	The trained system that uses data, parameters, and neural networks to perform tasks such as prediction, classification, and generation.
AI Translator Architecture Family	Language Conversion System	Systems that transform input into output, enabling AI to convert text, speech, or images into meaningful responses.
AI Agent Family	Action and Task Execution System	AI systems designed to perceive information, make decisions, and carry out tasks autonomously or semi-autonomously.
Chip Family	Hardware Brain	Physical processors (GPUs, TPUs, CPUs, NPUs) that perform AI computations.
Watts Family	Energy Power	The electrical power required to run AI hardware and data centers.
AI Energy Family	Energy Source System	The total energy consumed over time to operate AI systems, including training and real-time usage.
Infrastructure Family	Global Support System	Data centers, internet networks, cloud systems, and global infrastructure that allow AI to operate and scale.
Ingredient Family	System Composition	The essential components that come together to create an AI system, including data, algorithms, models, hardware, and energy.
Qubit Family	Quantum Information Units	Quantum bits that can represent multiple states simultaneously, forming the foundation of quantum computing.

The Bit Family

Introduction

The Bit Family represents the starting point of all digital technology. Every computer system, application, and artificial intelligence model is built from bits—the smallest unit of information in computing.

A bit can hold one of two values: 0 or 1. While this may seem simple, these two values form the foundation of everything digital. When bits are combined and organized, they create larger units of data that allow computers to store text, display images, play videos, and run complex systems.

From a single bit to massive data systems, all digital information follows this same structure. This is how computers are able to represent and process the world in a form they can understand.

In artificial intelligence, bits are essential because they store the data that models learn from, process the calculations that drive decision-making, and support the systems that generate responses.

Understanding the Bit Family helps students see how simple binary signals grow into powerful technologies. It reveals that behind every advanced AI system is a foundation built from the most basic building blocks of information.

Bit Family — Visual Understanding of Data Size

How Much Data Can Each Unit Hold? (Simple Examples)

Unit	Size	Photos (Approx.)	Video (Approx. Hours)
Bit	1 bit	N/A	N/A
Byte	8 bits	1 character	N/A
Kilobyte (KB)	~1,000 bytes	Part of a paragraph	N/A
Megabyte (MB)	~1,000 KB	~1 photo	~1 minute of video
Gigabyte (GB)	~1,000 MB	~250 photos	~1–2 hours of video
Terabyte (TB)	~1,000 GB	~250,000 photos	~1,000–2,000 hours of video
Petabyte (PB)	~1,000 TB	~250 million photos	~1–2 million hours of video
Exabyte (EB)	~1,000 PB	~250 billion photos	~1–2 billion hours of video
Zettabyte (ZB)	~1,000 EB	~250 trillion photos	~1–2 trillion hours of video
Yottabyte (YB)	~1,000 ZB	~250 quadrillion photos	~1–2 quadrillion hours of video

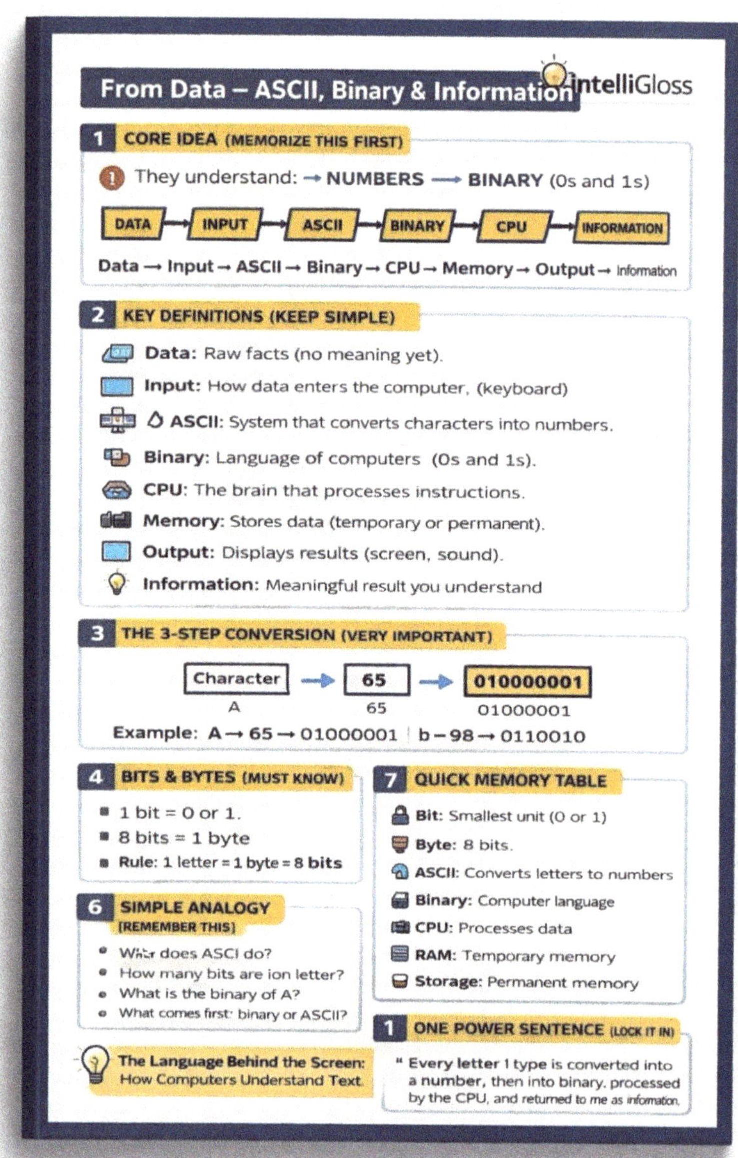

⚙ *The Algorithm Family*

Definition and Overview

The **Algorithm Family** represents the *thinking engine* of artificial intelligence — the set of mathematical instructions that guide how AI analyzes data, learns patterns, and makes decisions.

An **algorithm** is a sequence of steps designed to solve a problem or complete a task. In AI, algorithms tell the system *how to learn*, *how to predict*, and *how to improve* with every iteration.

In simple terms:

The Algorithm Family is the *logic of intelligence* — the invisible code that transforms data into decisions and predictions into progress.

🧠 How Algorithms Power AI

Every AI system — from simple chatbots to large-scale deep learning models — relies on algorithms as its foundation.
They determine how the model:

- Processes and cleans data,
- Identifies relationships between variables,
- Learns from feedback, and
- Improves over time.

Without algorithms, even the most powerful dataset or neural network would remain static and lifeless.

In essence, **algorithms are the teachers** that train AI how to think.

⚙️ *Why the Algorithm Family Matters*

Algorithms are what separate automation from intelligence.
They allow machines to **reason**, **adapt**, and **learn** — not just follow commands.
For prompt engineers, understanding algorithmic behavior helps explain *why* AI sometimes misunderstands a question, repeats patterns, or changes tone after feedback.

Every AI response you receive follows an underlying process — a pattern recognition journey from input to output.

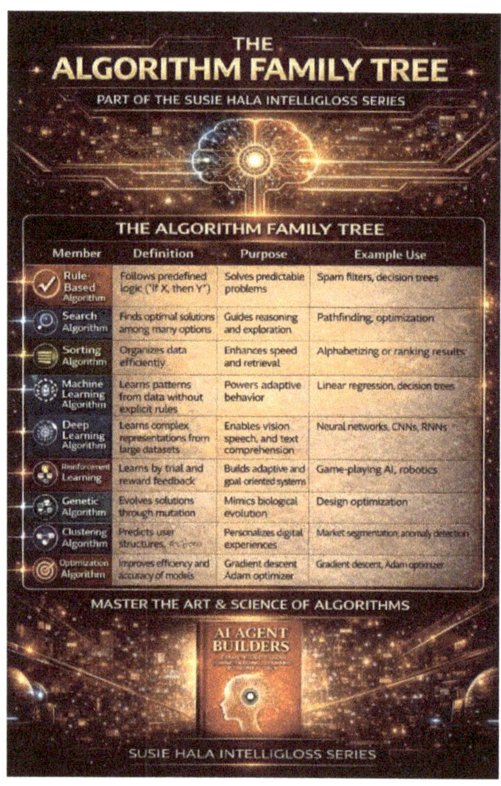

Member	Definition	Purpose	Example Use
Rule-Based Algorithm	Follows predefined logic ("If X, then Y")	Solves predictable problems	Spam filters, decision trees
Search Algorithm	Finds optimal solutions among many options	Guides reasoning and exploration	Pathfinding, optimization
Sorting Algorithm	Organizes data efficiently	Enhances speed and retrieval	Alphabetizing or ranking results
Machine Learning Algorithm	Learns patterns from data without explicit rules	Powers adaptive behavior	Linear regression, decision trees
Deep Learning Algorithm	Learns complex representations from large datasets	Enables vision speech, and text comprehension	Neural networks, CNNs, RNNs
Reinforcement Learning	Learns by trial and reward feedback	Builds adaptive and goal oriented systems	Game-playing AI, robotics
Genetic Algorithm	Evolves solutions through mutation	Mimics biological evolution	Design optimization
Clustering Algorithm	Predicts user structures,	Personalizes digital experiences	Market segmentation, anomaly detection
Optimization Algorithm	Improves efficiency and accuracy of models	Gradient descent Adam optimizer	Gradient descent, Adam optimizer

🌍 Analogy for Everyday Readers

Imagine AI as a chef in a kitchen:

The **Dataset Family** provides the ingredients.

The **Knowledge Family** gives the recipes.

The **Algorithm Family** is the *cooking process* — mixing, heating, tasting, and adjusting until the dish is perfect.

Just as cooking methods determine the quality of food, algorithms determine the quality of intelligence.

⚡ Algorithm Efficiency and Energy Use

Not all algorithms are equal.
Some are **fast but shallow**, while others are **deep but energy-intensive**.
Training large AI models requires algorithms that can handle billions of calculations per second — powered by the **Watts Family** (energy) and executed through the **Chip Family** (hardware).

The design of efficient algorithms directly affects sustainability in AI — minimizing power consumption while maximizing accuracy and speed.

🧩 Algorithms and Prompt Engineering

For prompt engineers, algorithms explain *how* the AI arrives at its answers.
When a model gives inconsistent or off-topic results, it's often due to:

Misinterpretation of input signals (input encoding),

Bias in training algorithms, or

Overfitting to certain data patterns.

Knowing this helps you craft prompts that guide the AI's decision-making — not just its output.

💬 **Quick Takeaway: The Algorithm Family is the reasoning heart of AI.**
It transforms information into understanding and enables machines to think, learn, and evolve like digital problem-solvers.

Absolutely, partner — this is a powerful section in your book because **tokens are where AI meets language**. I'll keep this aligned with your style: clear, structured, and school-district ready.

Token Family Introduction

The Token Family represents one of the most important bridges between human language and artificial intelligence. While humans communicate using words, sentences, and meaning, AI systems do not understand language in the same way. Instead, they rely on tokens—small units of text that allow machines to process, analyze, and generate language step by step.

A token can be a word, part of a word, a character, or even punctuation. When a student types a sentence into an AI system, that sentence is not read as a whole idea. It is first broken down into tokens. These tokens become the input that the AI model uses to recognize patterns, predict outcomes, and generate responses.

The Token Family works closely with several other foundational families in artificial intelligence. It connects directly with the Data Family, which provides the text used for training, and the Neural Network Family, which processes token patterns to produce intelligent outputs. It also plays a key role in the AI Translator Architecture Family, where tokens are transformed, analyzed, and reassembled into meaningful responses.

Understanding tokens helps students see what is happening behind the scenes when they interact with AI tools. Instead of viewing AI as a "magic system," they begin to understand that every response is built from sequences of tokens processed through mathematical models.

In simple terms, if language is what humans speak, tokens are what AI understands.

Token Family Breakdown Chart

Component	Role	Description	Example
Tokenization	Input Conversion	The process of breaking text into smaller units (tokens) that AI can process	"Artificial Intelligence" → "Artificial" + "Intelligence"
Tokens	Language Units	The individual pieces of text used by AI models for understanding and generation	"AI", "learn", "ing", "."
Subword Tokens	Efficiency Units	Words split into smaller parts to handle unknown or complex vocabulary	"unbelievable" → "un", "believ", "able"
Character Tokens	Fine-Grained Units	Text broken down into individual characters for detailed processing	"AI" → "A" + "I"
Vocabulary (Token Set)	Token Library	The complete set of tokens an AI model recognizes and uses	GPT models have thousands to millions of tokens
Encoding	Token Mapping	Converting tokens into numerical representations for computation	"AI" → [1234, 5678] (example IDs)
Decoding	Output Reconstruction	Converting numerical outputs back into readable text	[1234, 5678] → "AI system"
Context Window	Memory Limit	The number of tokens an AI can process at one time	Example: 8,000 tokens ≈ several pages of text
Token Embeddings	Meaning Representation	Mathematical vectors that capture relationships between tokens	"king" and "queen" have similar embeddings
Token Prediction	Language Generation	The process of predicting the next token in a sequence	"AI is" → predicts "powerful"

The Token Family reminds us that behind every intelligent response is a structured sequence of tokens working together. What feels like natural conversation to humans is, for AI, a carefully processed stream of language units transformed into meaning.

The AI Ecosystem Family

The AI Ecosystem Family is a connected group of artificial intelligence technologies, systems, behaviors, and applications that work together to help machines perform intelligent tasks. This ecosystem includes core AI systems, AI agents, agentic AI, AI autonomy, autonomous AI workers, and generative AI. Each part plays a different role in how modern AI systems think, learn, create, make decisions, solve problems, and interact with the world.

At the center of the ecosystem is artificial intelligence itself — the broad field focused on building machines and software that can perform tasks that normally require human intelligence. AI agents act as the systems that carry out goals and actions. Agentic AI describes the ability of AI systems to plan, reason, adapt, and pursue objectives with limited human guidance. AI autonomy represents the level of independence an AI system has while making decisions and taking actions. AI autonomous workers apply these capabilities to perform real-world tasks like digital employees or assistants. Generative AI adds the ability to create new content such as text, images, music, video, code, and designs.

The AI Ecosystem Family demonstrates that modern artificial intelligence is no longer just one single technology. Instead, it is an interconnected environment of systems, tools, intelligence, automation, creativity, and human collaboration. As AI continues to evolve, these technologies are becoming increasingly integrated into education, business, healthcare, communication, cybersecurity, research, and everyday life.

Understanding the AI Ecosystem Family helps students, educators, and readers see how the different parts of AI connect together to shape the future of intelligent systems and the digital world.

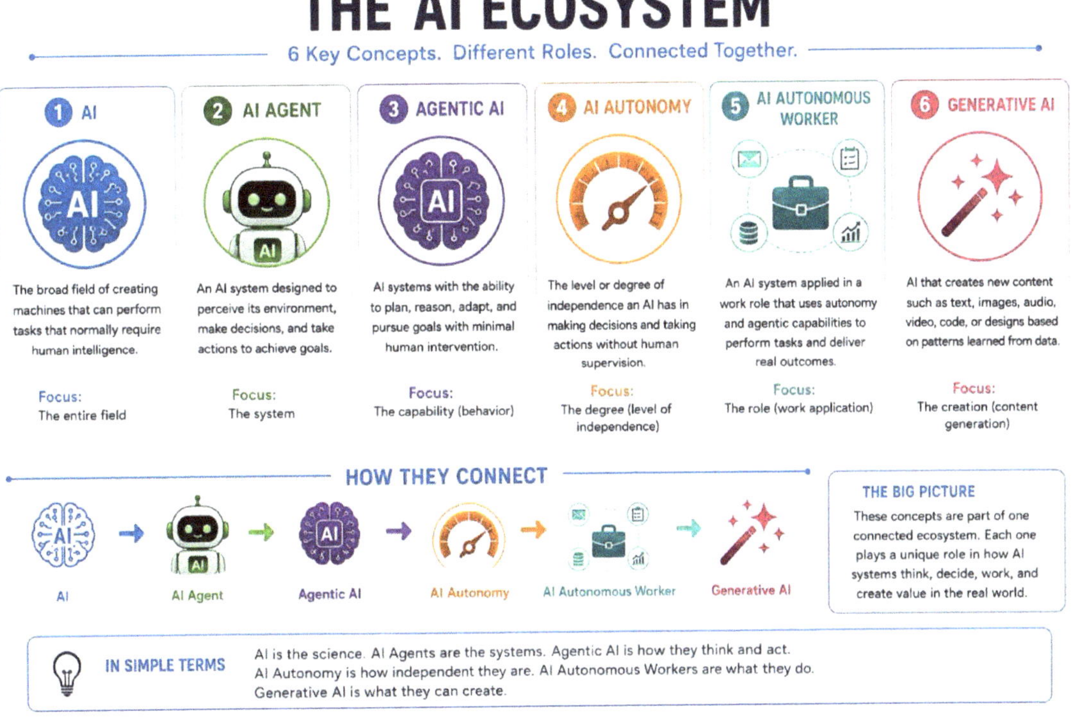

Parameter Family Introduction

The Parameter Family represents the internal learning system of artificial intelligence. While tokens provide the language and data provides the learning material, parameters are what allow AI systems to adjust, improve, and make intelligent decisions over time.

In simple terms, parameters are numerical values inside an AI model that change as the system learns. These values are not visible to users, but they play a critical role in how the model understands patterns, relationships, and meaning. Every time an AI system is trained, it adjusts its parameters to better predict outcomes and generate accurate responses.

Parameters exist throughout neural networks, where they act as the connections between artificial neurons. Each connection has a weight, which determines how important a particular piece of information is. During training, these weights are continuously adjusted based on data, allowing the system to improve its performance.

The Parameter Family works closely with the Data Family, which provides the information needed for learning, and the Neural Network Family, which organizes how parameters are structured and applied. It also supports the Token Family by helping the model interpret and predict sequences of language.

Understanding parameters helps students recognize that AI is not simply programmed with fixed rules. Instead, it learns by adjusting internal values that guide how it processes information. These adjustments are what allow AI systems to evolve from simple pattern recognition to complex reasoning and decision-making.

In essence, if data is what AI learns from, parameters are how AI learns.

Parameter Family Breakdown Chart

Component	Role	Description	Example
Parameters	Learning Values	Numerical values inside an AI model that are adjusted during training	Millions or billions of values inside a model
Weights	Connection Strength	Values that determine how strongly one neuron influences another	A higher weight = stronger influence
Bias	Adjustment Factor	A value added to help the model shift and fine-tune outputs	Helps improve accuracy in predictions
Training Process	Learning Mechanism	The process of adjusting parameters using data to improve performance	Model improves after analyzing many examples

Component	Role	Description	Example
Loss Function	Error Measurement	Measures how far the model's prediction is from the correct answer	Lower loss = better performance
Optimization Algorithm	Adjustment Strategy	Method used to update parameters efficiently	Gradient Descent adjusts weights step by step
Gradient	Direction of Change	Indicates how parameters should change to reduce error	Shows whether to increase or decrease a value
Backpropagation	Learning Process	System that sends error signals backward to update parameters	Adjusts earlier layers based on output error
Hyperparameters	Control Settings	External settings that guide how training happens (not learned)	Learning rate, batch size
Model Size	Capacity Indicator	The total number of parameters in a model	Larger models = more learning capacity

The Parameter Family is the hidden engine of learning in artificial intelligence. While users interact with outputs, it is the continuous adjustment of parameters behind the scenes that makes intelligent behavior possible.

Data Family Introduction

The Data Family represents the foundation of learning in artificial intelligence. Every AI system depends on data to develop knowledge, recognize patterns, and make decisions. Without data, artificial intelligence cannot learn, adapt, or function effectively.

Data can take many forms, including text, images, audio, video, and numerical information. These inputs provide the raw material that AI systems analyze during training. By studying large amounts of data, AI models begin to identify patterns, relationships, and structures that allow them to make predictions and generate responses.

The quality and diversity of data play a critical role in how well an AI system performs. Accurate, balanced, and relevant data helps models produce reliable results, while poor or biased data can lead to incorrect or unfair outcomes. This is why data collection, preparation, and evaluation are essential steps in the development of responsible AI systems.

The Data Family works closely with the Parameter Family, which adjusts internal values based on data, and the Neural Network Family, which processes and organizes data through layers of computation. It also supports the Token Family when dealing with language, as text data is converted into tokens for analysis.

Understanding the Data Family helps students recognize that AI does not "know" things on its own. Instead, it learns from the information it is given. The more meaningful and well-prepared the data, the more capable the AI system becomes.

In simple terms, data is the source of knowledge, and it is the starting point for all artificial intelligence.

Data Family Breakdown Chart

Component	Role	Description	Example
Data	Learning Material	Raw information used by AI systems to learn patterns and relationships	Text, images, audio, numbers
Dataset	Organized Collection	A structured group of data used for training and evaluation	A folder of labeled images
Training Data	Learning Input	Data used to teach the AI model during training	Thousands of sentences for a language model
Validation Data	Performance Check	Data used to tune the model during training without directly learning from it	Helps prevent overfitting
Test Data	Final Evaluation	Data used to measure how well the model performs after training	New unseen examples
Structured Data	Organized Format	Data arranged in tables with clear categories	Spreadsheets, databases
Unstructured Data	Flexible Format	Data without a predefined structure	Text documents, images, videos
Labeled Data	Guided Learning	Data tagged with correct answers to guide training	Image labeled "cat" or "dog"
Unlabeled Data	Self-Learning Input	Data without labels, used in unsupervised learning	Raw text without categories
Data Quality	Accuracy Measure	The reliability and correctness of data	Clean, complete, and consistent data
Data Bias	Imbalance Issue	When data does not represent all groups fairly	Skewed or incomplete datasets
Data Preprocessing	Preparation Step	Cleaning and organizing data before training	Removing errors, formatting text

The Data Family reminds us that artificial intelligence is only as strong as the information it learns from. High-quality data leads to meaningful insights, while poor data can limit or misguide intelligent systems.

Memory Family Introduction

The Memory Family represents how artificial intelligence systems store, retain, and retrieve information. Just as humans rely on memory to recall past experiences, learn new concepts, and make decisions, AI systems depend on memory to access previously processed information and maintain context.

In artificial intelligence, memory is not a single component but a collection of mechanisms that allow systems to handle information over time. Some forms of memory are short-term, holding information temporarily while a task is being completed. Other forms are long-term, storing learned knowledge that can be used across different tasks and interactions.

Memory plays a critical role in enabling AI systems to understand sequences, maintain context in conversations, and improve decision-making. For example, when a user interacts with a language model, the system uses memory to keep track of previous words, sentences, or prompts in order to generate coherent and relevant responses.

The Memory Family works closely with the Data Family, which provides the information to be stored, and the Parameter Family, which encodes learned knowledge within the model. It also supports the Neural Network Family by enabling systems to process sequences and retain important patterns over time.

Understanding the Memory Family helps students see that AI is not simply reacting to individual inputs in isolation. Instead, it relies on stored information and contextual awareness to produce meaningful and consistent outputs.

In simple terms, if data is what AI learns from, memory is how AI remembers and uses what it has learned.

Memory Family Breakdown Chart

Component	Role	Description	Example
Memory	Information Storage	The ability of an AI system to store and access information	Retaining previous inputs in a task
Short-Term Memory	Temporary Storage	Holds information for immediate processing	Keeping track of words in a sentence
Long-Term Memory	Persistent Storage	Stores learned knowledge for future use	Knowledge embedded in model parameters
Context Memory	Conversation Tracking	Maintains information within a specific interaction	Remembering earlier parts of a prompt
Working Memory	Active Processing	Handles information currently being used in computation	Processing a sequence step by step

Component	Role	Description	Example
External Memory	Extended Storage	Memory stored outside the model for retrieval	Databases, vector stores
Internal Memory	Embedded Knowledge	Information stored within the model itself	Learned patterns inside neural networks
Sequence Memory	Order Awareness	Tracks the order of inputs over time	Understanding sentence structure
Retrieval Mechanism	Access System	Retrieves stored information when needed	Searching relevant past data
Attention Mechanism	Focus System	Highlights important parts of memory for processing	Focusing on key words in a sentence
Memory Capacity	Storage Limit	The amount of information the system can handle at once	Context window size

The Memory Family shows that intelligence is not just about processing information in the moment, but about retaining, organizing, and using knowledge over time to create meaningful understanding.

Knowledge Family Introduction

The Knowledge Family represents how artificial intelligence organizes, connects, and uses information to create understanding. While data provides raw information and memory stores it, knowledge is what gives that information meaning and structure.

In artificial intelligence, knowledge is not simply a collection of facts. It is the result of identifying relationships, patterns, and connections within data. AI systems use knowledge to recognize concepts, make decisions, and generate meaningful responses. This allows machines to move beyond simple data processing and toward more intelligent behavior.

Knowledge can be represented in different ways within AI systems. Some forms are structured, such as databases and knowledge graphs, where relationships between concepts are clearly defined. Other forms are learned implicitly through neural networks, where patterns are encoded within parameters and used to guide predictions.

The Knowledge Family works closely with the Data Family, which provides the information needed to build knowledge, and the Memory Family, which stores and retrieves that information. It also connects with the Parameter Family, where learned knowledge is embedded within the model, and the Neural Network Family, which processes and organizes that knowledge.

Understanding the Knowledge Family helps students recognize that AI systems do not simply memorize information. Instead, they learn how pieces of information relate to one another, allowing them to interpret meaning, solve problems, and respond intelligently.

In simple terms, if data is information and memory stores it, knowledge is the understanding that makes it useful.

Knowledge Family Breakdown Chart

Component	Role	Description	Example
Knowledge	Understanding System	Organized information that allows AI to interpret meaning and make decisions	Recognizing relationships between concepts
Facts	Basic Information	Individual pieces of information stored within a system	"Water freezes at 0°C"
Relationships	Connection Mapping	Links between pieces of information that create meaning	"Teacher teaches student"
Knowledge Representation	Structure System	Methods used to organize and store knowledge in AI	Knowledge graphs, semantic networks
Knowledge Graph	Network Mapping	A structured representation of entities and their relationships	Google Knowledge Graph
Semantic Understanding	Meaning Interpretation	The ability to understand meaning behind words and data	Understanding synonyms and context
Inference	Reasoning Process	Drawing conclusions based on known information	If A = B and B = C, then A = C
Rules	Decision Framework	Logical guidelines used to make decisions	If temperature < 0°C → freeze
Ontology	Concept Framework	A structured system defining categories and relationships	Classification of animals
Explicit Knowledge	Direct Information	Clearly defined and stored knowledge	Rules, databases
Implicit Knowledge	Learned Patterns	Knowledge learned through experience and data	Patterns learned by neural networks
Knowledge Integration	System Coordination	Combining information from multiple sources	Merging text, images, and data

The Knowledge Family transforms information into understanding, allowing artificial intelligence to move beyond data and memory into meaningful reasoning and intelligent decision-making.

AI Model Family Introduction

The AI Model Family represents the core system within artificial intelligence that performs tasks such as prediction, classification, and content generation. It is the part of AI that users interact with, whether they are asking questions, generating images, or analyzing data.

An AI model is a trained system that has learned patterns from data. During training, the model processes large amounts of information and adjusts its internal parameters to improve accuracy. Once trained, the model can take new input and produce meaningful output based on what it has learned.

AI models can take many forms depending on their purpose. Some models are designed to recognize images, others to understand language, and others to make decisions or predictions. Large Language Models (LLMs), for example, are designed to process and generate human language by predicting sequences of tokens.

The AI Model Family works closely with the Data Family, which provides the learning material, and the Parameter Family, which stores learned patterns. It also relies on the Neural Network Family for structure and the Chip and Infrastructure Families for execution and deployment.

Understanding the AI Model Family helps students see that AI is not just a concept, but a working system that has been trained to perform specific tasks. It is the engine that transforms input into output.

In simple terms, if AI is the system, the model is the part that actually does the thinking and producing.

AI Model Family Breakdown Chart

Component	Role	Description	Example
AI Model	Core System	The trained system that performs tasks	Chatbot, image generator
Training	Learning Process	Process of teaching the model using data	Learning from datasets
Inference	Output Generation	Using the trained model to produce results	Answering a question
Model Architecture	Structural Design	Defines how the model is built	Neural networks, transformers
Parameters	Learned Values	Internal values adjusted during training	Billions of weights
Input Data	Entry Information	Data provided to the model for processing	User prompt
Output Data	Result	The response or prediction generated	AI-generated text
Model Types	Functional Categories	Different kinds of models for different tasks	Classification, generation
Fine-Tuning	Model Adjustment	Improving a model for specific tasks	Custom-trained AI

Component	Role	Description	Example
Pretrained Model	Base System	A model trained on large datasets before use	General-purpose AI
Evaluation	Performance Check	Measuring how well the model performs	Accuracy, loss metrics

The AI Model Family represents the working core of artificial intelligence, where learned patterns are transformed into meaningful actions, predictions, and responses.

Neural Network Family Introduction

The Neural Network Family represents the structural foundation of how artificial intelligence learns and processes information. Inspired by the human brain, neural networks are systems of interconnected units, often called neurons, that work together to analyze data, recognize patterns, and make decisions.

In artificial intelligence, a neural network is made up of layers. The input layer receives data, the hidden layers process that data, and the output layer produces a result. As information flows through these layers, the network applies mathematical transformations that allow it to detect patterns and relationships within the data.

Neural networks rely heavily on the Parameter Family, where weights and biases determine how strongly information flows between neurons. During training, these parameters are adjusted to improve the network's performance. The more the network learns, the better it becomes at recognizing patterns and making accurate predictions.

The Neural Network Family works closely with the Data Family, which provides the information needed for learning, and the Memory and Knowledge Families, which help store and organize learned information. It also supports the Token Family when processing language, allowing AI systems to interpret sequences of tokens in meaningful ways.

Understanding neural networks helps students see that AI is not simply following instructions. Instead, it is learning from examples and improving over time through layered processing and pattern recognition.

In simple terms, neural networks are the systems that allow AI to think, learn, and make sense of information.

Neural Network Family Breakdown Chart

Component	Role	Description	Example
Neural Network	Learning Structure	A system of interconnected neurons that processes data and learns patterns	Image recognition system
Neuron (Node)	Processing Unit	A basic unit that receives input, processes it, and passes output forward	A single calculation point
Input Layer	Data Entry Point	The first layer that receives raw data	Pixels of an image
Hidden Layers	Processing Layers	Intermediate layers that transform data and detect patterns	Feature detection layers
Output Layer	Result Generator	The final layer that produces predictions or decisions	"Cat" vs "Dog" classification
Weights	Signal Strength	Values that determine how strongly inputs influence outputs	Higher weight = stronger impact
Bias	Adjustment Value	Helps shift outputs to improve learning accuracy	Fine-tuning predictions
Activation Function	Decision Function	Determines whether a neuron should activate based on input	ReLU, Sigmoid
Forward Propagation	Data Flow	The process of passing input data through the network to produce output	Input → Hidden → Output
Backpropagation	Learning Process	Adjusts weights and biases based on error to improve performance	Correcting mistakes
Loss Function	Error Measurement	Calculates how far the output is from the correct answer	Prediction vs actual
Deep Neural Network	Advanced Structure	A network with many hidden layers for complex learning	Deep learning models

The Neural Network Family provides the structure that allows artificial intelligence to transform data into understanding, making it possible for machines to learn from experience and improve over time.

Dual Language System in Artificial Intelligence

Definition

The Dual Language System in Artificial Intelligence refers to the way AI communicates using two different forms of language at the same time: human language for interaction and machine language for internal processing.

Key Components

Human Language (Natural Language)
This is the language people use to communicate with AI, such as English, Spanish, Tongan, or Fijian. It includes words, sentences, and questions that users type or speak.

Machine Language (Numerical Representation)
This is how AI understands information internally. Words are converted into numbers called tokens and processed using mathematical models and algorithms.

How It Works (Step-by-Step)

A user enters a question in human language

The AI converts the words into numerical tokens

The AI processes the tokens using a neural network

The AI generates a response based on patterns and probabilities

The response is converted back into human language

Example

User Input:
"What is Artificial Intelligence?"

AI Process:

Converts words into numbers

Analyzes patterns from training data

Predicts the best possible answer

Output:
"Artificial Intelligence is the ability of machines to perform tasks that normally require human intelligence."

Why This Matters

Understanding the dual language system helps students realize that:

AI does not "think" like humans

AI translates language into math and back into language

Every interaction with AI is based on patterns, not emotions or understanding

Applications

Chatbots and virtual assistants

Language translation systems

Search engines

Voice recognition tools

Challenges

Misinterpretation of human language

Bias in language data

Lack of true understanding or reasoning

Summary

Artificial Intelligence works by translating human language into machine-readable data and then converting the results back into human language. This dual system allows AI to interact with people while operating through mathematical processes behind the scenes.

AI Translator Architecture Family Introduction

The AI Translator Architecture Family represents the system that transforms input into meaningful output in artificial intelligence. It acts as the bridge between what humans provide and what AI produces. Whether a user types a question, uploads an image, or speaks a command, this architecture is responsible for interpreting that input and generating a response.

In artificial intelligence, translation does not only mean converting one language to another. It refers to the broader process of transforming one form of information into another. For example, text can be translated into a response, speech can be converted into text, and images can be interpreted into descriptions. This transformation process is at the core of how modern AI systems function.

The AI Translator Architecture is built on multiple foundational families. It relies on the Token Family to break input into manageable units, the Neural Network Family to process patterns, and the Parameter Family to guide learning. It also uses knowledge and memory to maintain context and produce coherent results.

At the center of this architecture is the ability to encode and decode information. Encoding transforms input into a format the model can understand, while decoding converts processed information back into human-readable output. This continuous transformation allows AI systems to interact with users in a natural and meaningful way.

Understanding the AI Translator Architecture Family helps students see that AI is not simply responding randomly. Instead, it is systematically translating input into output through structured processes and learned patterns.

In simple terms, if tokens are the language pieces and neural networks are the brain, the AI Translator Architecture is the system that turns understanding into communication.

AI Translator Architecture Family Breakdown Chart

Component	Role	Description	Example
AI Translator Architecture	Transformation System	Converts input into meaningful output	Question → Answer
Input Processing	Data Intake	Receives and prepares user input for analysis	Text prompt entered by a user
Encoding	Input Conversion	Transforms input into numerical representations	Words → token IDs
Context Building	Meaning Formation	Organizes input into a structured understanding	Sentence context tracking
Sequence Processing	Order Handling	Maintains the correct order of information	Word sequence in a sentence
Attention Mechanism	Focus System	Identifies important parts of input data	Highlighting key words
Representation Layer	Feature Mapping	Converts data into internal representations for processing	Embeddings
Decoding	Output Generation	Converts processed data back into human-readable form	Token IDs → words
Output Generation	Response Creation	Produces the final answer or result	AI-generated response
Multimodal Translation	Cross-Format Processing	Translates between different types of data	Image → text description
Feedback Loop	Improvement Cycle	Uses results to refine future outputs	Model learning over time

The AI Translator Architecture Family shows that artificial intelligence is not just about understanding information, but about transforming it into meaningful communication that humans can use and interact with.

AI Architecture Family Introduction

The AI Architecture Family represents the overall design and structure of an artificial intelligence system. While individual families such as Data, Parameters, and Neural Networks explain how AI learns and processes information, the AI Architecture Family shows how all these components are organized and work together as a complete system.

In artificial intelligence, architecture refers to the blueprint that defines how data flows through a system, how components interact, and how decisions are produced. It determines how input is received, how it is processed, and how output is generated. A well-designed architecture allows AI systems to operate efficiently, scale to large problems, and produce reliable results.

AI architectures can vary depending on the type of system being built. Some are designed for image recognition, others for language processing, and others for decision-making or automation. Despite these differences, most architectures share common elements such as input layers, processing layers, memory components, and output mechanisms.

The AI Architecture Family connects all foundational families. It integrates the Data Family for input, the Token Family for language processing, the Neural Network Family for computation, the Parameter Family for learning, and the Memory and Knowledge Families for storing and organizing information. It also works closely with the AI Translator Architecture Family to transform input into meaningful output.

Understanding the AI Architecture Family helps students see the "big picture" of artificial intelligence. Instead of viewing AI as separate parts, they begin to understand it as a coordinated system where each component plays a specific role.

In simple terms, if individual families are the parts of AI, the AI Architecture Family is the blueprint that brings everything together into one working system.

AI Architecture Family Breakdown Chart

Component	Role	Description	Example
AI Architecture	System Blueprint	The overall design that defines how an AI system is structured and operates	ChatGPT system design

Component	Role	Description	Example
Input Layer	Data Entry Point	Receives raw input from users or external sources	Text prompt, image upload
Preprocessing Layer	Data Preparation	Cleans and organizes input data before processing	Tokenization, normalization
Processing Core	Computation Engine	The main system where data is analyzed and transformed	Neural networks, transformers
Parameter System	Learning Core	Stores adjustable values that guide learning and predictions	Model weights and biases
Memory System	Context Storage	Maintains and retrieves information during processing	Context window, external memory
Knowledge System	Understanding Layer	Organizes relationships and meaning within the system	Knowledge graphs, learned patterns
Decision Layer	Output Logic	Determines the final output based on processed data	Selecting the best response
Output Layer	Result Delivery	Presents results to the user in a usable format	Text, image, or audio response
Feedback Loop	Improvement System	Uses outcomes to refine future performance	Model updates and retraining
Scalability System	Expansion Capability	Allows the system to handle increasing data and complexity	Cloud-based AI systems
Integration Layer	System Connection	Connects AI with external tools and platforms	APIs, databases, applications

The AI Architecture Family reveals that artificial intelligence is not a single technology, but a coordinated system of interconnected components working together to transform data into intelligent outcomes.

Chip Family Introduction

The Chip Family represents the physical hardware that powers artificial intelligence systems. While software components such as data, algorithms, and neural networks define how AI works, none of these systems can function without the computing chips that perform the actual calculations.

Chips are specialized electronic components designed to process information at extremely high speeds. In artificial intelligence, these chips handle the complex mathematical operations required for training models and generating outputs. Every prediction, calculation, and response produced by an AI system is executed by hardware within the Chip Family.

Different types of chips are used depending on the needs of the system. Central Processing Units (CPUs) handle general-purpose tasks, while Graphics Processing Units (GPUs) are optimized for parallel processing, making them ideal for training neural networks. More specialized chips, such as Tensor Processing Units (TPUs) and Neural Processing Units (NPUs), are designed specifically for AI workloads, enabling faster and more efficient computation.

The Chip Family works closely with the Neural Network Family, which defines the structure of computation, and the Parameter Family, which stores the values being processed. It also connects to the Infrastructure Family, where large-scale systems of chips are organized in data centers and cloud environments.

Understanding the Chip Family helps students recognize that artificial intelligence is not purely abstract. It depends on physical machines that require power, resources, and engineering to operate. These chips are the engines that bring AI models to life.

In simple terms, if AI is the intelligence, chips are the machines that make that intelligence possible.

Chip Family Breakdown Chart

Component	Role	Description	Example
Chip (Processor)	Computation Engine	Electronic hardware that performs calculations required for AI	CPU, GPU
CPU (Central Processing Unit)	General Processor	Handles a wide range of computing tasks	Running basic applications
GPU (Graphics Processing Unit)	Parallel Processor	Processes many calculations at once, ideal for AI training	Training neural networks
TPU (Tensor Processing Unit)	AI Accelerator	Specialized chip designed for machine learning tasks	Google TPU
NPU (Neural Processing Unit)	Edge AI Processor	Optimized for running AI on devices like phones	Smartphone AI features
AI Accelerator	Performance Booster	Hardware designed to speed up AI computations	Dedicated AI chips
Memory (Hardware)	Data Storage	Stores data and instructions for processing	RAM, VRAM
Parallel Processing	Speed Mechanism	Ability to perform multiple calculations simultaneously	GPUs processing thousands of operations
Throughput	Processing Capacity	Amount of data processed over time	High-performance computing systems
Latency	Response Time	Time it takes to process a request	Faster chips = lower latency
Power Consumption	Energy Usage	Amount of energy required to run the chip	High-performance GPUs use more power

Component	Role	Description	Example
Edge Devices	Local Processing	Devices that run AI locally without cloud support	Phones, smart cameras

The Chip Family reminds us that behind every intelligent system is powerful hardware performing millions or billions of calculations, turning abstract models into real-world functionality.

Watts Family Introduction

The Watts Family represents the measurement of power used by artificial intelligence systems. While the Chip Family provides the hardware that performs computations, the Watts Family explains how much energy those systems consume while operating.

A watt is a unit of power that measures the rate at which energy is used. In artificial intelligence, watts help us understand how much electricity is required to run processors, train models, and generate responses. Every time an AI system processes data, performs calculations, or produces output, it consumes power.

Different AI systems require different levels of power depending on their size and complexity. Small systems, such as those running on mobile devices, use relatively low amounts of power. In contrast, large-scale AI models operating in data centers can require significant amounts of electricity, especially during training, where billions of calculations are performed continuously.

The Watts Family works closely with the Chip Family, which determines how efficiently computations are performed, and the Infrastructure Family, where large networks of machines operate together. It also connects to the overall design of AI systems, as more efficient models can reduce power consumption while maintaining performance.

Understanding the Watts Family helps students recognize that artificial intelligence is not only about intelligence and computation, but also about energy use and resource management. As AI continues to grow, managing power efficiently becomes an important part of building responsible and sustainable systems.

In simple terms, if chips perform the work, watts measure how much power it takes to do that work.

Watts Family Breakdown Chart

Component	Role	Description	Example
Watt (W)	Power Measurement	Unit that measures the rate of energy use	A device using 100 watts
Power Consumption	Energy Usage Rate	Amount of power used during operation	AI model running on GPUs
Energy Efficiency	Performance Balance	How effectively a system uses power to perform tasks	More output with less power
High-Performance Computing	Intensive Power Use	Systems that require large amounts of power for complex tasks	AI training clusters
Idle Power	Standby Usage	Power consumed when systems are not actively processing	Servers waiting for requests
Peak Power	Maximum Usage	Highest level of power used during heavy workloads	Training large AI models
Thermal Output	Heat Generation	Heat produced as a result of power usage	Cooling systems in data centers
Cooling Systems	Temperature Control	Systems used to manage heat from high power usage	Air or liquid cooling
Power Supply	Energy Source	Provides electricity to AI systems	Electrical grid, batteries
Edge Power Usage	Local Energy Use	Power consumption on smaller devices	Smartphones, IoT devices
Data Center Power	Large-Scale Usage	Power required for large AI operations	Server farms running AI models
Sustainable Energy	Efficiency Goal	Use of renewable energy to reduce environmental impact	Solar-powered data centers

The Watts Family highlights that intelligence comes with a cost—every AI system requires power, and understanding that power is essential for building efficient and sustainable technologies.

Watts Family (AI Power Usage Scale)

Definition

The **Watts Family** represents the real-time power usage of artificial intelligence systems, measured in watts (W). It shows how much power AI systems consume at a given moment as they process data and perform computations.

Watts Scale

1 Watt
10 Watts

100 Watts
500 Watts
1,000 Watts (1 Kilowatt)
10,000 Watts (10 Kilowatts)
100,000 Watts (100 Kilowatts)
1,000,000 Watts (1 Megawatt)
10,000,000 Watts (10 Megawatts)
100,000,000+ Watts (100+ Megawatts)

Key Characteristics

Measured in real-world electrical power

Higher watt values indicate higher processing demand

Used to represent the scale of AI systems from small devices to large infrastructures

Closely connected to the Chip Family, Energy Family, and Infrastructure Family

Examples

Low watts → small devices and basic AI functions

Medium watts → computers and advanced applications

High watts → data centers and large AI systems

Summary

The **Watts Family** provides a numerical representation of how much power artificial intelligence systems use in real time, helping to illustrate the scale and intensity of AI operations.

🧠 Student Insight

Watts show how much power AI is using right now.

AI Energy Family Introduction

The AI Energy Family represents the total amount of energy consumed by artificial intelligence systems over time. While the Watts Family measures the rate at which power is used at any given moment, the Energy Family focuses on the accumulated energy required to perform tasks, run systems, and sustain operations.

In artificial intelligence, energy is used every time a model is trained, a system processes data, or a response is generated. Large-scale AI systems, especially those operating in data centers, can consume significant amounts of energy due to the continuous processing of massive datasets and complex computations.

Energy is typically measured over time using units such as kilowatt-hours (kWh), which reflect how much power has been used during a specific period. For example, running a high-performance AI system for several hours or days results in a total energy cost that goes beyond the moment-to-moment power usage measured in watts.

The AI Energy Family works closely with the Watts Family, which provides the rate of power consumption, and the Chip Family, which determines how efficiently computations are performed. It also connects to the Infrastructure Family, where large-scale systems operate continuously and require long-term energy management.

Understanding the AI Energy Family helps students recognize that artificial intelligence has real-world resource implications. It is not only about performance and speed, but also about sustainability, efficiency, and responsible use of technology.

In simple terms, if watts measure how fast energy is used, energy measures how much is used over time.

AI Energy Family Breakdown Chart

Component	Role	Description	Example
Energy	Total Consumption	The total amount of power used over a period of time	Running an AI system for hours or days
Kilowatt-hour (kWh)	Energy Measurement	Unit used to measure energy consumption over time	1 kWh = using 1,000 watts for 1 hour
Energy Usage	Consumption Tracking	Total energy required for AI operations	Training a large model
Training Energy	Learning Cost	Energy used during model training processes	Weeks of GPU usage
Inference Energy	Response Cost	Energy used when AI generates outputs	Answering a user prompt
Energy Efficiency	Optimization Goal	Reducing energy use while maintaining performance	Efficient AI models
Energy Scaling	Growth Impact	Increase in energy use as systems grow larger	Bigger models = more energy
Data Center Energy	Infrastructure Demand	Total energy used by large AI facilities	Server farms operating 24/7

Component	Role	Description	Example
Cooling Energy	Temperature Control	Energy required to cool systems and prevent overheating	Air conditioning in data centers
Renewable Energy	Sustainability Source	Use of clean energy to power AI systems	Solar, wind-powered data centers
Carbon Impact	Environmental Effect	Emissions associated with energy consumption	AI training carbon footprint
Energy Management	Resource Control	Strategies to monitor and reduce energy use	Efficient scheduling, hardware optimization

The AI Energy Family reminds us that artificial intelligence operates within the physical world, where every computation consumes energy and every system has an impact on resources and sustainability.

Energy Family (Total Power Consumption of Artificial Intelligence)

Definition

The **Energy Family** represents the total amount of electricity used by artificial intelligence systems over time. It is measured in watt-hours (Wh) or kilowatt-hours (kWh) and shows how much energy AI systems consume while running.

Energy Scale

1 Watt-hour (Wh)
10 Watt-hours (Wh)
100 Watt-hours (Wh)
500 Watt-hours (Wh)
1,000 Watt-hours (1 Kilowatt-hour, kWh)
10,000 Watt-hours (10 kWh)
100,000 Watt-hours (100 kWh)
1,000,000 Watt-hours (1 Megawatt-hour, MWh)
10,000,000 Watt-hours (10 MWh)
100,000,000+ Watt-hours (100+ MWh)

Key Characteristics

Measured over time (not instant like watts)

Represents total electricity consumption

Increases the longer AI systems run

Directly related to cost and energy usage

Closely connected to Watts Family, Chip Family, and Infrastructure Family

Examples

Low energy → short AI tasks or small devices

Medium energy → daily AI usage on computers

High energy → training AI models and running data centers

Summary

The **Energy Family** provides a numerical representation of the total electricity consumed by artificial intelligence systems over time, helping to illustrate the overall cost and impact of AI operations.

🧠 Student Insight

Energy shows how much total power AI has used over time.

AI Infrastructure Family Introduction

The AI Infrastructure Family represents the large-scale systems and environments that support, power, and connect artificial intelligence technologies. While individual components such as chips, data, and models explain how AI works, infrastructure explains where and how these systems operate in the real world.

AI infrastructure includes data centers, cloud platforms, networking systems, and storage environments that allow artificial intelligence to function at scale. These systems provide the computing power, data access, and connectivity needed to train models, process information, and deliver results to users around the world.

Modern AI systems rely heavily on cloud-based infrastructure, where thousands of machines work together to handle massive workloads. This allows AI to scale efficiently, making it possible to process large datasets, run complex models, and serve millions of users simultaneously. Infrastructure also ensures reliability, security, and continuous availability of AI services.

The AI Infrastructure Family works closely with the Chip Family, which provides the hardware, the Watts and Energy Families, which manage power consumption, and the Data Family, which supplies the information being processed. It also supports the AI Architecture Family by providing the environment where all system components are deployed and connected.

Understanding the AI Infrastructure Family helps students recognize that artificial intelligence is not contained within a single device. Instead, it operates across global systems that require coordination, resources, and engineering to function effectively.

In simple terms, if AI is the system and chips are the engines, infrastructure is the environment that allows everything to run at scale.

AI Infrastructure Family Breakdown Chart

Component	Role	Description	Example
AI Infrastructure	System Environment	The physical and digital systems that support AI operations	Global AI platforms
Data Center	Processing Hub	Facilities that house servers and computing equipment	Large server farms
Cloud Computing	Scalable Platform	Remote systems that provide computing resources over the internet	AWS, Azure, Google Cloud
Servers	Compute Units	Machines that process data and run AI models	Rack-mounted servers
Networking	Connectivity System	Systems that allow communication between machines	Internet, fiber networks
Storage Systems	Data Management	Systems that store large volumes of data	Databases, cloud storage
Distributed Computing	Workload Sharing	Splitting tasks across multiple machines for efficiency	Parallel processing across clusters
Edge Infrastructure	Local Processing	Running AI closer to the user or device	Smart devices, IoT systems
Load Balancing	Traffic Control	Distributes workloads to prevent overload	Managing user requests
Security Systems	Protection Layer	Safeguards data and systems from threats	Encryption, firewalls
Redundancy	Reliability System	Backup systems to ensure continuous operation	Failover servers
Scalability	Growth Capability	Ability to expand resources as demand increases	Adding more servers dynamically

The AI Infrastructure Family reveals that artificial intelligence operates on a global scale, relying on interconnected systems that provide the power, storage, and connectivity needed to support intelligent technologies.

AI Agent Family Introduction

The AI Agent Family represents systems that can take action, make decisions, and perform tasks on behalf of users or other systems. Unlike traditional AI models that only respond to input, AI agents are designed to operate with a level of autonomy, allowing them to plan, execute, and adapt to achieve specific goals.

An AI agent receives input from its environment, processes that information, and takes actions based on predefined objectives or learned behaviors. These actions can include answering questions, automating workflows, retrieving information, or interacting with other systems. Some agents operate in simple environments, while others function in complex systems that require continuous decision-making.

AI agents often combine multiple foundational families. They use the Data Family to gather information, the Memory and Knowledge Families to retain and understand context, and the Neural Network and Parameter Families to process and learn from interactions. They also rely on the AI Architecture and Infrastructure Families to operate reliably at scale.

Modern AI agents can work independently or as part of larger systems. For example, a customer support agent can respond to inquiries automatically, while a more advanced agent can complete multi-step tasks such as scheduling, research, or system management.

Understanding the AI Agent Family helps students see that artificial intelligence is not only about generating responses, but also about taking meaningful action in real-world scenarios.

In simple terms, if AI models think and respond, AI agents act and execute.

AI Agent Family Breakdown Chart

Component	Role	Description	Example
AI Agent	Action System	An AI system that can make decisions and perform tasks	Virtual assistant
Environment	Operating Context	The space where the agent interacts and gathers information	Web, apps, databases
Input Perception	Data Intake	Receives information from the environment	User query or sensor input

Component	Role	Description	Example
Decision Engine	Action Selection	Determines what action to take based on input	Choosing a response or task
Action Execution	Task Performance	Carries out decisions in the environment	Sending an email, retrieving data
Goal System	Objective Setting	Defines what the agent is trying to achieve	Complete a task or solve a problem
Planning Module	Strategy Builder	Breaks down tasks into steps	Multi-step problem solving
Feedback Loop	Learning Cycle	Improves performance based on outcomes	Adjusting actions over time
Autonomy Level	Independence Scale	Degree of independence in decision-making	Fully automated vs assisted
Multi-Agent System	Collaboration Network	Multiple agents working together	Coordinated AI systems

Ingredient Family Introduction

The Ingredient Family represents the essential components that come together to create an artificial intelligence system. Just as a recipe requires specific ingredients to produce a final dish, AI systems rely on a combination of foundational elements working together to function effectively.

Artificial intelligence is not built from a single component. It requires data to learn from, algorithms to guide processing, models to perform tasks, hardware to execute computations, and energy to power the entire system. Each of these elements plays a critical role, and the absence of any one component would prevent the system from operating properly.

The Ingredient Family provides a simplified way for students to understand AI as a system made up of interconnected parts. Instead of viewing AI as complex or mysterious, learners can begin to see it as something constructed from identifiable and understandable components.

This family connects directly with all other foundational families, including Data, Algorithm, Neural Network, Parameter, Chip, and Energy Families. It serves as an overview that brings these elements together into a unified perspective.

Understanding the Ingredient Family helps students recognize that artificial intelligence is built, not magical. It is the result of carefully combining the right components in the right way.

In simple terms, if AI is the final product, the Ingredient Family represents everything needed to build it.

Ingredient Family Breakdown Chart

Component	Role	Description	Example
Data	Learning Input	Provides the information AI uses to learn patterns	Text, images, audio
Algorithms	Instruction Set	Guides how data is processed and decisions are made	Sorting, classification
AI Models	Execution System	Performs tasks such as prediction or generation	Language models
Neural Networks	Processing Structure	Organizes how data is processed through layers	Deep learning models
Parameters	Learning Adjustments	Fine-tune how the model learns and makes predictions	Weights and biases
Tokens	Language Units	Breaks text into smaller pieces for processing	Words or subwords
Hardware (Chips)	Computation Engine	Executes calculations required by AI systems	GPUs, CPUs
Energy	Power Source	Supplies the energy needed to run systems	Electricity usage
Infrastructure	Support System	Provides the environment for AI to operate at scale	Cloud systems, data centers
Memory	Storage System	Stores and retrieves information for processing	Context memory
Knowledge	Understanding Layer	Represents meaning and relationships within data	Knowledge graphs

The Ingredient Family shows that artificial intelligence is built from a combination of essential components, each playing a vital role in creating intelligent systems.

The Frontend and Backend Family of Artificial Intelligence

How AI Systems Connect User Interaction to Intelligent Processing

Introduction

Every artificial intelligence system operates through two essential layers: the frontend and the backend. These layers work together to transform human interaction into intelligent responses, allowing AI systems to function smoothly and effectively.

The frontend is the part of the system that users see and interact with. It includes screens, input tools, and the display of results. Whether a user is typing a question, speaking a command, or uploading an image, all interaction begins at the frontend.

Behind the scenes, the backend serves as the processing engine of the system. It receives input from the frontend, manages data, connects to the AI model, and performs the computations needed to generate a response. The backend is where the intelligence of the system operates, using models, algorithms, and infrastructure to interpret and respond to user requests.

This visual illustrates how these two layers work together as a complete system. It shows the flow of information from user input to AI processing and back to the user as a result. By understanding this structure, students can see that AI is not a single tool, but a coordinated system of layers working together.

In simple terms, the frontend is where interaction happens, and the backend is where intelligence is created.

Every AI system has two sides: what you see and what actually does the thinking.

AI Qubit Family Introduction

The AI Qubit Family represents the foundation of quantum computing as it relates to artificial intelligence. While traditional computing relies on bits, which can exist as either 0 or 1, quantum computing uses qubits, which can exist in multiple states simultaneously.

A qubit is the basic unit of quantum information. Unlike classical bits, qubits can take advantage of properties such as superposition and entanglement, allowing quantum systems to process complex computations more efficiently in certain scenarios. This opens new possibilities for solving problems that are difficult or impossible for traditional computers.

In the context of artificial intelligence, qubits have the potential to accelerate learning processes, optimize large-scale systems, and improve complex simulations. Although quantum AI is still in development, it represents a future direction where computational power can expand beyond current limitations.

The AI Qubit Family connects with the Chip Family, as quantum processors are specialized hardware, and with the Algorithm Family, where new types of quantum algorithms are designed. It also relates to the Parameter and Neural Network Families, as researchers explore quantum-enhanced learning models.

Understanding the AI Qubit Family helps students see that artificial intelligence is continuously evolving. It introduces the idea that the foundations of computing themselves can change, leading to new forms of intelligence and problem-solving.

In simple terms, if bits are the foundation of today's computing, qubits represent the foundation of tomorrow's possibilities.

AI Qubit Family Breakdown Chart

Component	Role	Description	Example
Qubit	Quantum Unit	Basic unit of quantum information	Quantum bit in a quantum computer
Superposition	Multi-State Ability	Ability to exist in multiple states at once	0 and 1 simultaneously
Entanglement	Connection Property	Linking qubits so they influence each other	Paired quantum states
Quantum Gate	Operation System	Performs operations on qubits	Quantum logic gates
Quantum Circuit	Processing Structure	Sequence of quantum operations	Quantum algorithms
Quantum Processor	Hardware Engine	Specialized chip for quantum computing	Quantum computer hardware
Quantum Algorithm	Computation Method	Algorithm designed for quantum systems	Optimization problems
Quantum Speedup	Performance Advantage	Faster processing for certain problems	Complex simulations
Quantum Noise	Stability Challenge	Errors caused by environmental interference	Qubit instability
Quantum Error Correction	Stability Solution	Techniques to reduce errors in quantum systems	Fault-tolerant computing

The AI Qubit Family introduces a new frontier in computing, where the limits of traditional systems are expanded, opening the door to more powerful and advanced forms of artificial intelligence.

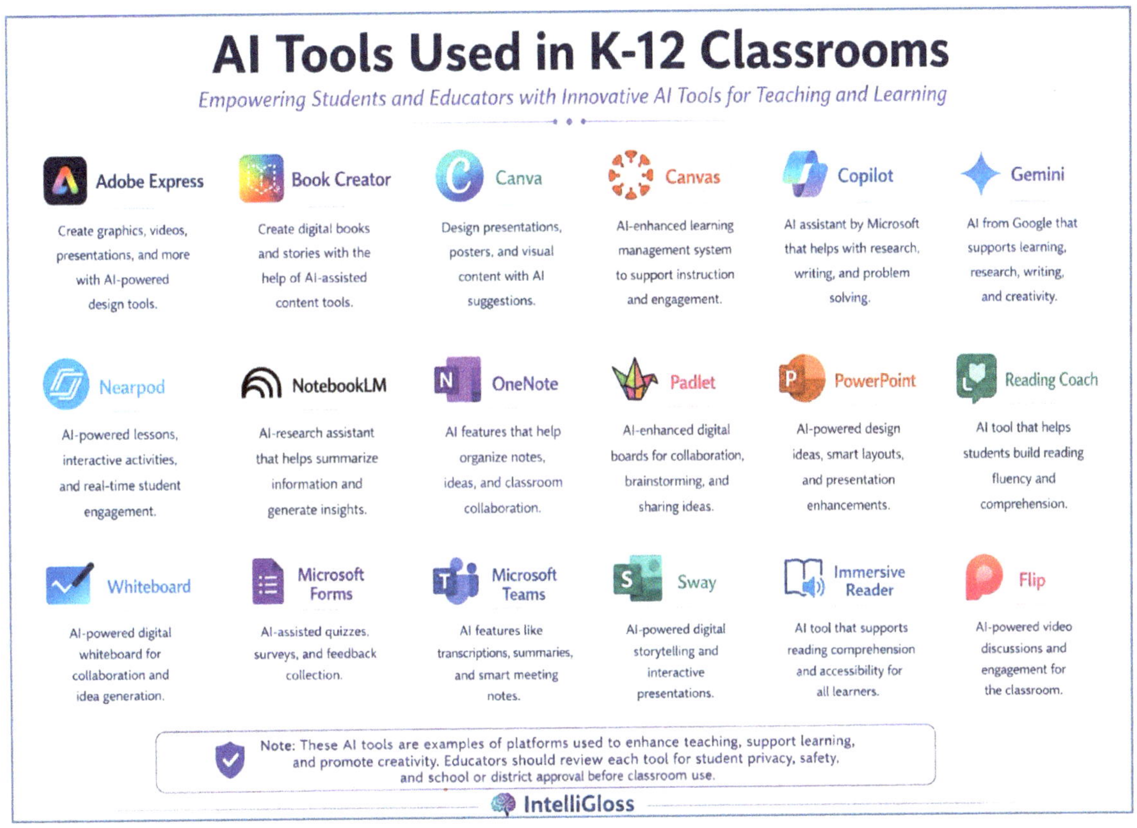

TITLE: The Data Center: The Engine Behind Artificial Intelligence

Table of Contents

Data Drives Decisions in Every Industry

TITLE: The Data Center: The Engine Behind Artificial Intelligence

Introduction

Why Data Drives Decisions in Every Industry

We live in a world shaped by decisions. Every day, decisions are made about education, healthcare, business, transportation, safety, technology, and even our homes. Some decisions are small and personal, while others affect entire communities, organizations, and nations. What many people do not realize is that behind almost every modern decision lies one powerful force: **data**.

Data is the quiet foundation of the digital age. It is collected when students take exams, when doctors review medical records, when businesses track sales, when cities manage traffic, and when families use smartphones and smart devices. Although data often remains invisible to the people affected by it, it plays a central role in shaping outcomes, opportunities, and future directions.

This book begins with a simple but important idea: **data does not exist for its own sake**. Data exists to inform decisions. When data is accurate, timely, and responsibly used, it helps individuals and organizations make better choices. When data is incomplete, biased, outdated, or misunderstood, it can lead to poor decisions, wasted resources, and serious harm. Understanding this difference is essential in today's world.

Across every industry, data has become a decision-making tool. In education, data helps teachers understand how students learn and where support is needed. In healthcare, data guides diagnoses, treatments, and life-saving research. In business, data influences pricing, inventory, hiring, and long-term planning. In government, data shapes policies, public services, and infrastructure. Even in everyday life, data affects what we see online, how our homes operate, and how technology responds to our needs.

Yet despite its importance, data is often misunderstood. Many people assume data is only for scientists, programmers, or technology companies. Others see data as overwhelming numbers or technical charts with little relevance to daily life. This book challenges those assumptions. It presents data as something **everyone interacts with**, whether they realize it or not, and something **everyone should understand at a basic level**.

The purpose of this book is not to teach readers how to code or perform advanced analytics. Instead, it aims to explain **how data flows through systems**, how it influences decisions, and why responsible data use matters across industries. By focusing on real-world examples and clear explanations, this book helps readers see the connection between information and action.

As artificial intelligence, automation, and digital systems continue to grow, data literacy is becoming as essential as reading and math. People who understand how data is collected, interpreted, and applied are better prepared to question decisions, protect their privacy, and participate responsibly in a data-driven society. This is especially important for students, parents, educators, business owners, and community leaders who will shape the next generation of decisions.

Data Drives Decisions in Every Industry is written to empower readers with understanding, not fear. It explains how data supports progress while also addressing the ethical responsibilities that come with its use. By the end of this book, readers will see data not as an abstract concept, but as a practical force that influences nearly every aspect of modern life.

This introduction marks the starting point of that journey. The chapters that follow will explore how data works, where it appears across industries, and why informed decision-making depends on it more than ever before.

Chapter 1

What Data Really Is (And What It Is Not)

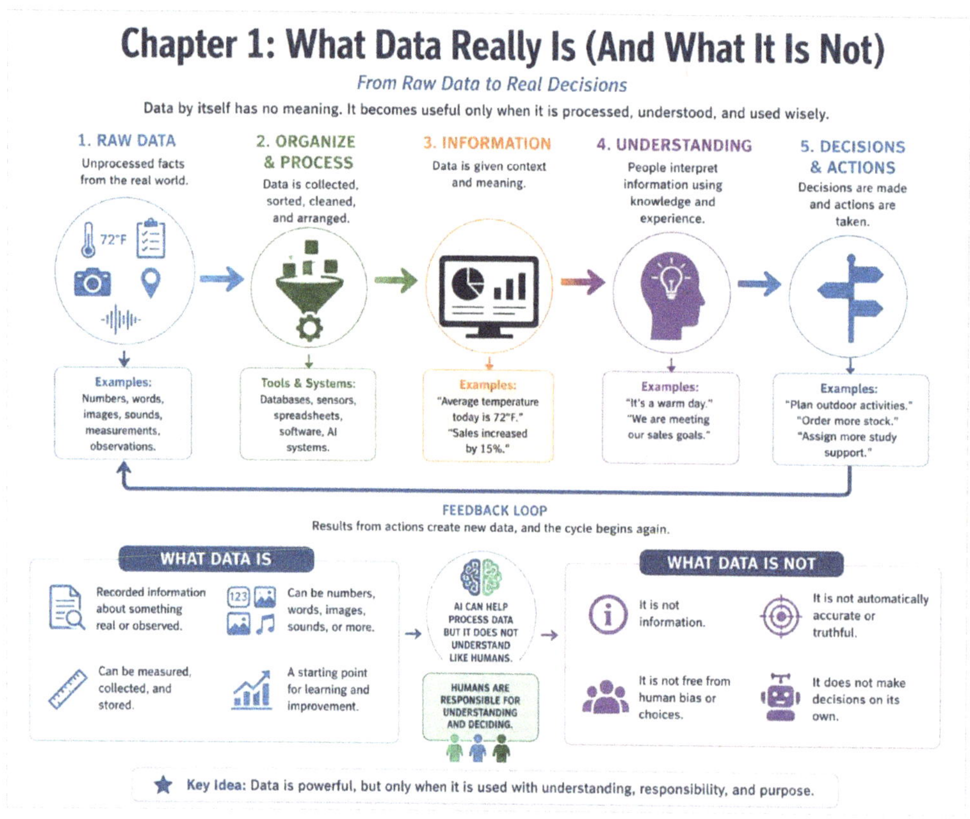

Before understanding how data drives decisions, it is important to understand **what data actually is**. The word "data" is used so often in modern conversations that it can lose its meaning. People hear it in schools, businesses, hospitals, news reports, and technology discussions, yet many still feel uncertain about what counts as data and why it matters.

At its core, **data is recorded information**. It can take many forms, but its purpose is always the same: to describe something that has happened, is happening, or might happen in the future. Data can represent numbers, words, images, sounds, measurements, movements, or patterns. Whenever something is observed, measured, or captured in a recordable way, data is being created.

Data exists long before computers. Weather logs, attendance sheets, medical charts, receipts, maps, and census records are all examples of data that existed well before the digital age. What has changed is **the speed, scale, and complexity** at which data is now collected and used. Modern systems can capture millions of data points in seconds, allowing decisions to be made faster and across wider systems than ever before.

It is important to understand that **data is not the same as information**. Data is raw and unprocessed. It does not explain itself. For example, a list of test scores, temperatures, or sales numbers is data. On its own, it does not tell a story. When data is organized, analyzed, and given context, it becomes information. When that information is understood and applied, it supports decisions.

Data is also not the same as intelligence. Intelligence involves judgment, reasoning, and interpretation. Machines and systems do not possess understanding in the human sense. They rely on data to detect patterns and make predictions, but humans remain responsible for deciding how those outputs are used. This distinction is essential, especially as artificial intelligence becomes more common in everyday systems.

Another common misunderstanding is the belief that data is always objective. In reality, data reflects **human choices**. People decide what to collect, how to measure it, what to include, and what to exclude. These choices can introduce gaps, bias, or limitations. For example, if data is collected from only one group, one location, or one time period, it may not represent the full picture. Understanding this helps readers question decisions instead of blindly accepting them.

Data can be qualitative or quantitative. Quantitative data involves numbers and measurements, such as prices, scores, distances, or time. Qualitative data involves descriptions, opinions, observations, and categories, such as survey responses, written feedback, or interview transcripts. Both types of data are valuable, and many real-world decisions rely on a combination of the two.

In the digital age, data is created constantly. Each time a student logs into a learning platform, a patient visits a clinic, a customer makes a purchase, or a phone tracks location for directions, data is generated. Often this happens automatically, without users actively thinking about it. This makes understanding data even more important, because decisions can be influenced quietly and at scale.

Data by itself has no meaning and no intention. It does not decide, judge, or act. It must be interpreted within a system and applied by people or automated processes. When data is misunderstood, ignored, or misused, decisions suffer. When it is carefully collected, responsibly handled, and thoughtfully interpreted, it becomes one of the most powerful tools available to modern society.

This chapter establishes a foundation: data is not mysterious, magical, or reserved for experts. It is a basic building block of modern systems. In the next chapter, we will explore **how data moves from raw records to real-world decisions**, and why that process matters across every industry

What Data Really Is (And What It Is Not)

Chapter Summary

This chapter explains what data truly is and clears up common misunderstandings about how it is used. Data is defined as recorded information that represents observations, measurements, or events. It can exist in many forms, including numbers, words, images, sounds, and patterns. Data has existed long before computers, but modern technology allows it to be collected and processed much faster and on a much larger scale.

The chapter emphasizes that data is not the same as information or intelligence. Data is raw and unprocessed. When data is organized and analyzed, it becomes information. Intelligence involves reasoning and judgment, which machines do not possess in the human sense. Humans remain responsible for interpreting data and making decisions based on it.

Another key idea is that data is not always objective. Human choices affect what data is collected and how it is used, which can introduce bias or limitations. The chapter also explains the difference between quantitative data (numbers and measurements) and qualitative data (descriptions and observations), showing that both are important. Overall, the chapter establishes data as a foundational building block of modern systems and prepares students to understand how data influences decisions.

Quiz: Chapter 1

Instructions: Choose the best answer or respond briefly.

1. What is data at its most basic level?
2. Which of the following is an example of data that existed before computers?
   a) Social media analytics
   b) Weather logs
   c) AI model predictions
   d) Automated sensors
3. Why is data not the same as information?
4. What happens when data is organized and analyzed?
5. Why is data not the same as intelligence?
6. True or False: Data always explains itself clearly.
7. What does quantitative data focus on?

8. What is an example of qualitative data?
9. Why can data contain bias?
10. Why is understanding data important in the digital age?

Worksheet: Understanding Data

Part A: Concept Check

1. In your own words, define **data**.
2. List three different forms data can take.
3. Explain the difference between **data** and **information**.

Part B: Think & Apply

4. Give one real-life example of data you generate in a normal day.
5. Explain how that data might be used to make a decision.
6. Why is it important for humans to remain responsible for decisions made using data?

Part C: Critical Thinking

7. Describe a situation where data might not show the full picture.
8. Why is it important to understand both qualitative and quantitative data?
9. What could happen if data is misunderstood or misused?
10. Write one question you would ask before trusting data used in a decision.

Answer Key

Quiz Answers

1. Data is recorded information.
2. **b) Weather logs**
3. Data is raw and unprocessed, while information is organized and given context.
4. It becomes information that can support decisions.
5. Intelligence involves judgment and reasoning, which data alone does not have.
6. **False**
7. Numbers and measurements
8. Survey responses, written feedback, or interviews
9. Because humans decide what to collect, include, or exclude
10. Because data is constantly collected and used to influence decisions

Worksheet Sample Answers

Part A

1. Data is information that has been recorded through observation or measurement.

2. Numbers, words, images (other answers acceptable).
3. Data is raw facts; information is data that has been organized and interpreted.

Part B

4. Logging into a school platform, making a purchase, using GPS (answers vary).
5. It can be used to track performance, improve services, or make predictions.
6. Because machines do not understand meaning or consequences.

Part C

7. Data collected from only one group or time period may not represent everyone.
8. Because numbers show trends and descriptions provide context and meaning.
9. Poor or harmful decisions could be made.
10. Who collected this data and why? (answers may vary)

Chapter 2

Where Data Comes From

To understand how data drives decisions, it is essential to understand **where data comes from**. Data does not appear on its own. It is created through observation, measurement, interaction, and recording. Every piece of data has an origin, and knowing that origin helps people judge how reliable, complete, and useful the data may be.

Data is generated whenever something is observed or tracked. In everyday life, this can happen intentionally or automatically. When a teacher records attendance, data is created. When a doctor measures blood pressure, data is created. When a business records a sale, data is created. Even when a phone tracks steps, location, or app usage, data is being generated quietly in the background.

One of the most common sources of data is **human activity**. Forms, surveys, applications, exams, interviews, and feedback all produce data. Schools collect data through grades, assessments, and attendance records. Businesses collect data through customer purchases, service requests, and support interactions. Governments collect data through census surveys, permits, and public records. In these cases, data reflects human behavior, choices, and responses.

Another major source of data comes from **machines and sensors**. Modern systems rely heavily on devices that collect data automatically. Sensors measure temperature, motion, light, sound, pressure, speed, and location. Cameras capture images and video. Microphones record sound. Smart meters track electricity and water usage. These sources generate large volumes of data quickly and consistently, often without human input after setup.

Digital platforms are also powerful data generators. Websites, mobile apps, learning platforms, and online services collect data whenever users interact with them. Clicking a link, watching a video, submitting a form, or making a purchase all create data points. Over time, these interactions form patterns that organizations use to understand behavior, improve services, and make predictions.

Data also comes from **systems and processes**. Inventory systems track stock levels. Transportation systems record routes and traffic flow. Financial systems record transactions, budgets, and payments. Healthcare systems track patient histories and treatment outcomes. In these cases, data is created as part of routine operations, not as a separate activity.

It is important to recognize that data can be collected **actively or passively**. Active data collection happens when people knowingly provide information, such as filling out a form or answering a survey. Passive data collection happens when systems collect information automatically, such as location tracking or usage statistics. Both methods are widely used, and both raise important questions about transparency and consent.

Not all data is collected for the same purpose. Some data is gathered to solve immediate problems, such as identifying a student who needs support or restocking a product that is running low. Other data is collected for long-term analysis, planning, or research. Understanding the original purpose of data helps determine whether it should be used in new or different ways.

Another key factor is **data context**. Data collected in one situation may not apply well to another. For example, data collected during an unusual event, such as a natural disaster or economic crisis, may not represent normal conditions. Using data without understanding its context can lead to incorrect conclusions and poor decisions.

Data sources are expanding rapidly as technology evolves. Smart cities, autonomous systems, wearable devices, and artificial intelligence platforms all rely on continuous data streams. As a result, organizations now manage not just data points, but entire data ecosystems made up of multiple sources working together.

Understanding where data comes from helps readers become more informed participants in a data-driven world. It allows them to ask important questions: Who collected this data? How was it collected? Why was it collected? What might be missing? These questions are essential for responsible decision-making.

In the next chapter, we will explore **how raw data is transformed into meaningful insights**, and how that transformation supports decisions across every industry.

Do AI Companies Buy Data or Subscribe to Data?

The short answer:
AI companies **buy data**, **subscribe to data**, **license data**, **collect their own data**, and **partner for data**. Most use **a combination**, not just one method.

Data is valuable, and how it is obtained matters legally, ethically, and financially.

Buying Data (One-Time or Bulk Purchases)

Some AI companies **buy datasets outright**. This usually happens when the data is:

- Historical
- Structured
- Curated
- Hard to collect independently

Examples include:

- Medical imaging datasets
- Financial market histories
- Satellite imagery archives
- Language corpora
- Annotated images or videos

When data is bought, the company typically gains **limited usage rights**, not full ownership like physical property. Contracts define:

- How the data can be used
- Whether it can train AI models
- Whether it can be resold
- How long it can be used

Buying data is common when companies need **large volumes quickly**.

Subscribing to Data (Ongoing Access)

Many AI companies **subscribe to live or regularly updated data streams**. This is extremely common.

Subscription data includes:

- Financial market feeds
- Weather data
- Traffic and mapping data
- News and content feeds
- Consumer behavior analytics
- Business intelligence platforms

With subscriptions:

- The data is **never owned**
- Access continues only while payments continue
- Data is constantly refreshed

This is ideal for AI systems that require **real-time or near-real-time decisions**, such as trading systems, logistics optimization, or fraud detection.

Licensing Data (Very Common in AI)

Licensing is one of the **most important and misunderstood methods**.

In licensing:

- The data owner keeps ownership
- The AI company pays for **permission to use the data**
- Usage is strictly defined

Licenses may allow:

- Model training
- Testing and validation
- Internal research only
- Commercial deployment

Licensing is widely used for:

- Books and written content
- Academic research datasets
- Media archives
- Proprietary business data

This is where many legal and ethical debates around AI exist today.

Collecting Their Own Data

Many large AI companies collect **their own data** through:

- Platforms (search engines, apps, tools)
- User interactions
- Sensors and devices
- Voluntary submissions

Examples:

- Search queries
- Voice assistants learning speech patterns
- Navigation apps learning traffic patterns
- Chat systems learning language structure

This data is usually governed by:

- User agreements
- Privacy policies
- Data protection laws

This method gives companies **continuous, scalable data**, but also carries the **highest responsibility** for privacy and security.

Data Partnerships and Sharing Agreements

Some AI companies **do not buy or subscribe**, but instead **partner**.

In partnerships:

- One organization provides data
- Another provides technology or analysis
- Both benefit

Examples:

- Hospitals partnering with AI research firms
- Cities partnering with traffic optimization companies
- Universities partnering with AI labs

These agreements often include:

- Strict anonymization rules
- Oversight committees
- Shared intellectual property terms

Why AI Companies Use Multiple Data Sources

No single data source is enough.

AI systems need:

- Historical data to learn patterns
- Live data to stay accurate
- Diverse data to reduce bias
- Verified data to ensure reliability

That's why modern AI systems are built on **data ecosystems**, not single datasets.

Where Data Comes From

Chapter Summary

This chapter explains how data is created and where it comes from. Data does not appear on its own; it is generated through observation, measurement, interaction, and recording. Every piece of data has an origin, and understanding that origin helps people judge how reliable, complete, and appropriate the data may be for decision-making.

The chapter explores multiple sources of data, including human activity, machines and sensors, digital platforms, and operational systems. Schools, businesses, governments, and healthcare organizations all generate data as part of everyday processes. Modern technology has expanded data collection through automated sensors, smart devices, and online interactions, creating large and continuous data streams.

The chapter also explains the difference between active and passive data collection, emphasizing the importance of transparency and consent. It highlights why data purpose and context matter, noting that data collected for one situation may not apply well to another. Finally, the chapter introduces how AI companies obtain data—through buying, subscribing, licensing, collecting their own data, and forming partnerships—showing that modern AI systems rely on complex data ecosystems rather than a single source.

Quiz: Chapter 2

Instructions: Answer the questions below.

1. Why is it important to understand where data comes from?
2. Give one example of data created through human activity.
3. What role do sensors play in data generation?
4. How do digital platforms create data?
5. What is the difference between active and passive data collection?
6. True or False: All data is collected for the same purpose.
7. Why does data context matter when making decisions?
8. Name two ways AI companies can obtain data.
9. What is one risk of using data without understanding how it was collected?
10. Why do AI systems rely on multiple data sources instead of just one?

Worksheet: Exploring Data Sources

Part A: Understanding the Basics

1. Define **data source** in your own words.
2. List three different places data can come from.
3. Explain how data can be generated without people actively noticing it.

Part B: Real-World Application

4. Identify one example of data you generate at school or home.

5. Is this data collected actively or passively? Explain.
6. How might this data be used to make a decision?

Part C: AI & Data Collection

7. Explain the difference between **buying data** and **subscribing to data**.
8. Why is licensing data common in AI development?
9. Give one example of a data partnership.
10. Why is it important for AI companies to use diverse data sources?

Answer Key

Quiz Answers

1. It helps determine how reliable, complete, and appropriate the data is.
2. Grades, surveys, forms, or attendance records (answers may vary).
3. Sensors automatically measure and record information such as temperature or movement.
4. Through user interactions like clicks, views, submissions, and purchases.
5. Active collection is when people knowingly provide data; passive collection happens automatically.
6. **False**
7. Because data collected in one situation may not represent normal conditions.
8. Buying, subscribing, licensing, collecting their own data, or partnerships.
9. It can lead to incorrect conclusions or poor decisions.
10. Because no single source provides enough accuracy, diversity, or reliability.

Worksheet Sample Answers

Part A

1. A data source is where information is created or collected.
2. People, machines/sensors, digital platforms (other answers acceptable).
3. Devices like phones and apps collect data automatically in the background.

Part B

4. Logging into a learning platform or using a navigation app.
5. Passive, because it is collected automatically (answers may vary).
6. It can be used to track performance, improve services, or plan resources.

Part C

7. Buying data is a one-time or bulk purchase; subscribing provides ongoing access.
8. Because it allows controlled use of valuable data without transferring ownership.
9. A hospital partnering with an AI research firm (answers may vary).
10. To reduce bias, improve accuracy, and ensure reliable AI performance.

Chapter 3

Buying Data and Subscribing to Data

In the modern digital economy, data has become a resource that organizations actively seek, manage, and invest in. While some data is collected internally, many organizations—including artificial intelligence companies—also rely on **externally sourced data**. Two of the most common ways this happens are through **buying data** and **subscribing to data**. Understanding the difference between these approaches helps explain how data-driven systems operate and why data access is carefully controlled.

Buying data refers to acquiring a dataset through a one-time or limited purchase. In this model, an organization pays for access to a specific collection of data that already exists. This data may be historical, curated, or specially prepared for analysis. For example, a company might purchase years of weather records, medical images for research, or labeled images used to train visual recognition systems. Buying data allows organizations to quickly access large volumes of information without having to collect it themselves.

However, buying data does not usually mean full ownership in the traditional sense. Instead, the purchase typically includes **usage rights** defined by legal agreements. These agreements specify how the data can be used, whether it can be shared, how long it can be retained, and whether it can be used to train artificial intelligence systems. This ensures that the original data owner maintains control while allowing the buyer to benefit from the information.

Subscribing to data works differently. Rather than receiving a fixed dataset, organizations pay for **ongoing access** to data that is continuously updated. Subscription-based data is especially valuable when decisions depend on current or real-time information. Financial markets, traffic systems, weather services, and supply chains often rely on subscribed data streams to stay accurate and responsive.

In a subscription model, data is never owned by the subscriber. Access exists only as long as the subscription remains active. Once the subscription ends, the right to use the data typically ends as well. This model encourages organizations to treat data as a service rather than a product, ensuring that decisions are based on the most up-to-date information available.

Both buying and subscribing to data play important roles in artificial intelligence systems. Purchased datasets help train models by providing large amounts of historical examples. Subscribed data helps keep those models relevant by feeding them fresh inputs. Together, these approaches allow systems to learn from the past while responding to the present.

The choice between buying and subscribing to data depends on purpose. Data that changes slowly, such as archived records or labeled training datasets, is often purchased. Data that changes rapidly, such as live sensor readings or financial prices, is usually subscribed to. In many cases, organizations use both methods at the same time, creating layered data environments.

Ethical and legal considerations are central to both approaches. Data agreements must respect privacy laws, consent requirements, and usage limitations. Sensitive data, such as health or personal information, often includes strict protections to prevent misuse. Responsible organizations establish governance policies to ensure data is handled transparently and securely.

Understanding how data is acquired also helps individuals become more informed participants in the digital world. When people know that data can be bought or subscribed to under legal agreements, they gain insight into how systems make decisions and why accountability matters. This awareness supports trust, regulation, and responsible innovation.

Buying data and subscribing to data are not shortcuts or hidden practices. They are structured, regulated processes that reflect the growing importance of data as a shared resource. As industries continue to rely on intelligent systems, these methods of accessing data will remain essential to how decisions are made.

In the next chapter, we will explore **how data quality and accuracy affect decisions**, and why even the best data sources can lead to poor outcomes if not carefully managed.

Buying Data and Subscribing to Data

Chapter Summary

This chapter explains two common ways organizations obtain external data: **buying data** and **subscribing to data**. As data becomes a valuable resource in the digital economy, many organizations—especially those using artificial intelligence—rely on these methods to access information they cannot easily collect on their own.

Buying data involves a one-time or limited purchase of an existing dataset, often historical or carefully prepared. This allows organizations to quickly access large volumes of information, such as past records or labeled examples used for training AI systems. However, buying data usually does not mean full ownership. Instead, usage rights are defined by legal agreements that specify how the data can be used, shared, or stored.

Subscribing to data provides ongoing access to continuously updated information. This model is commonly used when decisions depend on real-time or frequently changing data, such as weather, traffic, or financial markets. In subscription models, data is treated as a service rather than a product, and access ends when the subscription ends.

The chapter highlights how buying and subscribing to data serve different purposes but are often used together. Purchased data helps systems learn from the past, while subscribed data helps them respond to the present. Ethical and legal responsibilities, including privacy, consent, and transparency, are essential in both approaches. Understanding these methods helps readers become more informed and responsible participants in a data-driven world.

Quiz: Chapter 3

Instructions: Answer the following questions.

1. What does it mean to buy data?
2. Why do organizations buy historical datasets?
3. Does buying data usually mean full ownership? Explain briefly.
4. What does subscribing to data provide that buying data does not?
5. Give one example of data that is commonly subscribed to.
6. True or False: Subscribed data can usually be used forever once accessed.
7. How do buying and subscribing to data support AI systems differently?
8. Why are legal agreements important when acquiring data?
9. What type of data is more likely to be purchased rather than subscribed to?
10. Why is understanding data acquisition important for individuals?

Worksheet: Understanding Data Access Models

Part A: Key Concepts

1. In your own words, explain the difference between **buying data** and **subscribing to data**.
2. List two examples of data that might be bought.
3. List two examples of data that might be subscribed to.

Part B: Think & Apply

4. Imagine a company developing a navigation app.
   - Which type of data would it likely subscribe to?
   - Why?
5. Imagine a research project studying climate trends over 50 years.
   - Would buying or subscribing to data make more sense? Explain.

Part C: Responsibility & Ethics

6. Why is it important to protect privacy when buying or subscribing to data?
7. What could happen if data usage rules are ignored?
8. Explain why data is considered a service in subscription models.
9. Why might an organization use both purchased and subscribed data at the same time?
10. Write one question you would ask about data before trusting decisions made from it.

Answer Key

Quiz Answers

1. Buying data means paying for access to a specific dataset, usually through a one-time or limited purchase.
2. To quickly access large volumes of existing information without collecting it themselves.

3. No. Buying data usually includes limited usage rights defined by legal agreements.
4. Ongoing access to updated or real-time information.
5. Weather data, traffic data, or financial market data.
6. **False**
7. Purchased data helps train models using historical examples, while subscribed data keeps models updated with current information.
8. They define how data can be used, shared, stored, and protected.
9. Historical records or labeled training datasets.
10. It helps people understand how systems make decisions and why accountability matters.

Worksheet Sample Answers

Part A

1. Buying data provides a fixed dataset, while subscribing provides ongoing access to updated data.
2. Historical weather records, medical images, archived reports.
3. Traffic data, stock prices, live sensor data.

Part B

4. Traffic and location data, because it changes constantly and must be current.
5. Buying data, because the focus is on long-term historical trends.

Part C

6. To prevent misuse of sensitive or personal information.
7. Legal consequences, loss of trust, or harm to individuals.
8. Because access depends on continued payment and data is constantly refreshed.
9. To combine historical learning with real-time decision-making.
10. Who collected this data and for what purpose? (answers may vary)

Chapter 4

How Data Is Stored

Chapter 4: How Data Is Stored

From Creation to Safe Use

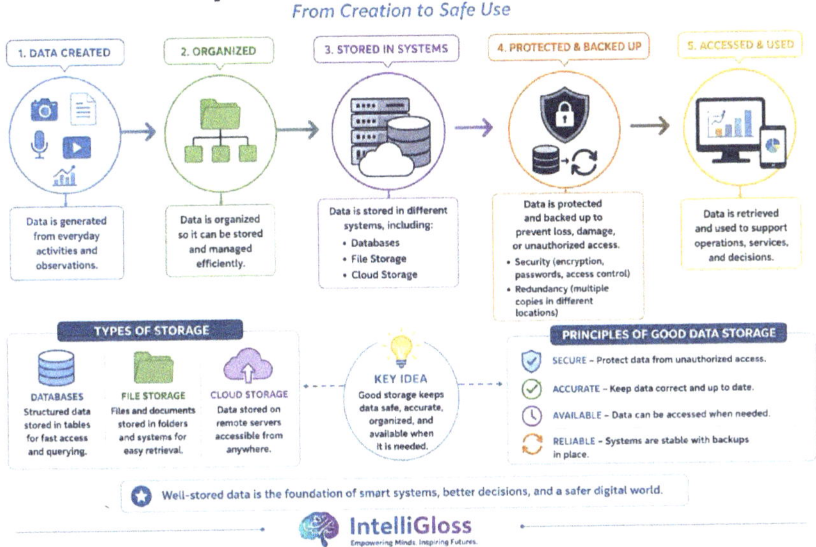

Once data is collected, it must be stored in a way that allows it to be accessed, protected, and used effectively. Data storage is a critical part of modern systems because decisions cannot be made if data is lost, corrupted, or unavailable. Across every industry, the way data is stored directly affects reliability, security, and long-term success.

At its most basic level, storing data means keeping recorded information in a place where it can be retrieved later. Historically, this meant filing cabinets, paper records, and physical archives. Today, most data is stored digitally, allowing it to be searched, copied, analyzed, and shared at high speed. Digital storage has transformed how organizations operate, but it has also introduced new responsibilities.

Modern data is commonly stored in **databases**. A database is an organized digital system designed to hold large amounts of data in a structured way. Databases allow information to be updated, queried, and managed efficiently. Schools use databases to store student records. Hospitals store patient information in medical databases. Businesses store customer, inventory, and financial data in specialized database systems.

In addition to databases, many organizations rely on **file-based storage systems**. These systems store documents, images, videos, and other files in organized digital folders. File storage is useful for materials such as reports, scanned documents, training videos, and media content. While simpler than databases, file storage still requires careful organization and access control.

As data volumes grow, organizations increasingly use **cloud storage**. Cloud storage allows data to be stored on remote servers managed by specialized providers. Instead of maintaining physical servers on-site, organizations access data through secure internet connections. Cloud storage offers flexibility, scalability, and redundancy, making it especially valuable for growing businesses, schools, and public institutions.

Another important concept in data storage is **data redundancy**. This means keeping multiple copies of data in different locations. Redundancy protects against data loss caused by hardware failure, natural disasters, or cyberattacks. Backup systems and recovery plans ensure that critical data can be restored if something goes wrong.

Security is a central concern in how data is stored. Stored data must be protected from unauthorized access, alteration, or theft. This is achieved through encryption, access controls, authentication systems, and monitoring tools. Sensitive data, such as personal, financial, or medical information, often requires higher levels of protection due to legal and ethical obligations.

Data storage is not only about keeping information safe, but also about keeping it **usable**. Poorly organized data can become difficult to find, interpret, or trust. For this reason, organizations establish data management policies that define how data is labeled, updated, archived, and eventually deleted. These policies help ensure that stored data remains accurate and relevant over time.

Another challenge is deciding **how long data should be stored**. Some data must be retained for legal or regulatory reasons, while other data loses value over time. Storing data indefinitely can increase costs and risks, especially if outdated information is misused. Responsible storage includes deciding when data should be archived or securely removed.

As artificial intelligence systems rely more heavily on stored data, storage decisions become even more important. AI models depend on historical data to learn patterns and on accessible storage systems to retrieve information efficiently. Poor storage practices can limit system performance or introduce errors into decision-making processes.

Understanding how data is stored helps readers appreciate the unseen infrastructure supporting modern life. Data storage is not a passive activity; it is an active process that requires planning, responsibility, and ongoing maintenance. When data is stored thoughtfully, it becomes a reliable foundation for informed decisions across every industry.

In the next chapter, we will explore **why data quality matters**, and how stored data must be accurate, complete, and trustworthy to truly support good decision-making.

How Data Is Stored

Chapter Summary

This chapter explains why data storage is an essential part of modern systems. Once data is collected, it must be stored so it can be accessed, protected, and used when needed. Without reliable storage, data can be lost, damaged, or unavailable, making informed decision-making impossible.

The chapter describes different ways data is stored, including databases, file-based storage systems, and cloud storage. Databases organize large amounts of structured information and are commonly used by schools, hospitals, and businesses. File storage systems hold documents, images, and media files in organized digital folders. Cloud storage allows organizations to store data on remote servers, offering flexibility, scalability, and backup protection.

Key concepts such as data redundancy, security, and data management policies are also introduced. Redundancy ensures multiple copies of data exist to prevent loss. Security measures protect stored data from unauthorized access or misuse. The chapter emphasizes that storing data is not only about safety, but also about keeping data organized, accurate, and useful over time. As artificial intelligence relies heavily on stored data, responsible storage practices play a critical role in system performance and decision quality.

Quiz: Chapter 4

Instructions: Answer the questions below.

1. Why is data storage important for decision-making?
2. What is the main purpose of a database?
3. Give one example of data commonly stored in a database.
4. How is file-based storage different from database storage?
5. What is cloud storage?
6. True or False: Data redundancy means storing only one copy of data.
7. Why are backups important in data storage systems?
8. Name one method used to protect stored data.
9. Why can poorly organized data be a problem?
10. How does data storage affect artificial intelligence systems?

Worksheet: Understanding Data Storage

Part A: Core Concepts

1. Define **data storage** in your own words.
2. List three different ways data can be stored.
3. Explain what data redundancy means and why it matters.

Part B: Real-World Connections

4. Give one example of data stored at school or at home.
5. Which type of storage would be best for this data? Explain why.
6. Why might an organization choose cloud storage instead of on-site servers?

Part C: Thinking Critically

7. Why is data security especially important for sensitive information?
8. What could happen if outdated data is stored and used incorrectly?
9. Why do organizations create rules for how long data is kept?
10. Write one question you would ask about how data is stored before trusting it.

Answer Key

Quiz Answers

1. Because decisions cannot be made if data is lost, damaged, or unavailable.
2. To organize and manage large amounts of structured data efficiently.
3. Student records, medical records, or customer information.
4. File-based storage stores documents and media files, while databases store structured data for querying and updates.
5. Data stored on remote servers accessed through the internet.
6. **False**
7. To restore data if it is lost due to failure, disaster, or attack.
8. Encryption, access controls, or authentication systems.
9. It can be difficult to find, understand, or trust the data.
10. AI systems rely on stored data to learn patterns and make accurate decisions.

Worksheet Sample Answers

Part A

1. Data storage is the process of keeping recorded information so it can be accessed later.
2. Databases, file storage systems, cloud storage.
3. It means keeping multiple copies of data to prevent loss.

Part B

4. Homework files, grades, photos, or financial records.
5. File storage or a database, depending on the type of data (answers may vary).
6. Because it offers scalability, flexibility, and backup protection.

Part C

7. Because sensitive data can cause harm if accessed or misused.
8. It could lead to incorrect decisions or confusion.
9. To meet legal requirements and reduce risks and costs.
10. Where is this data stored and who can access it? (answers may vary)

Chapter 5

Why Data Quality Matters

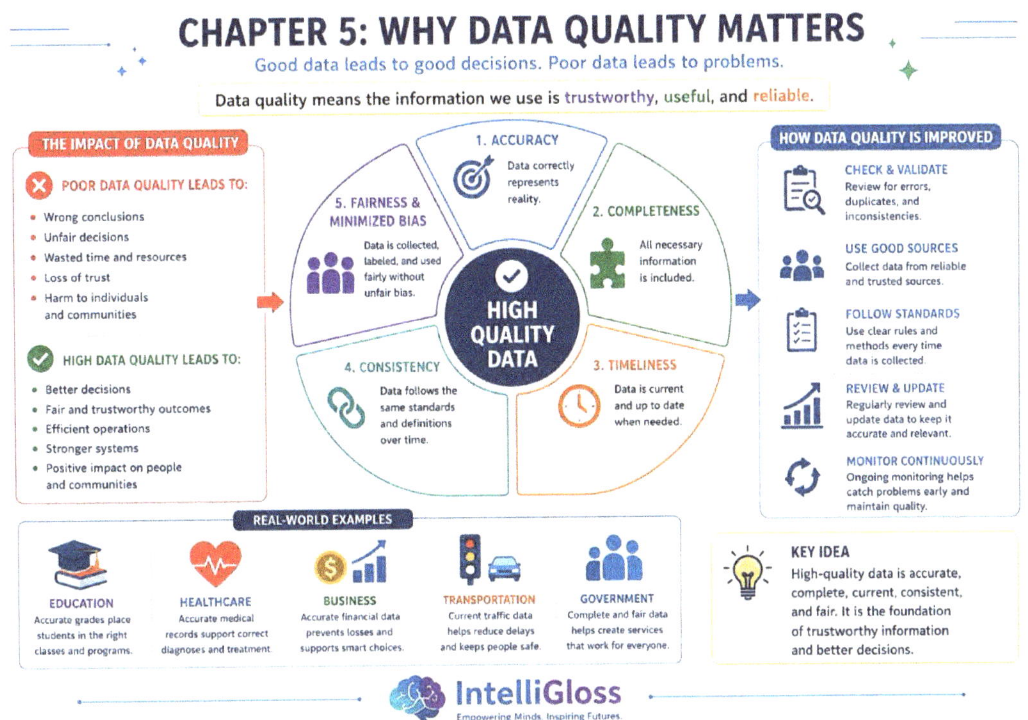

Storing data is only part of the responsibility. For data to truly support decisions, it must be **high quality**. Data quality determines whether information can be trusted, understood, and used effectively. Across every industry, poor data quality leads to poor decisions, no matter how advanced the technology or systems may be.

High-quality data is data that accurately represents reality. It reflects what actually happened, what is currently happening, or what conditions truly exist. When data is inaccurate, incomplete, outdated, or misleading, it can distort understanding and cause decisions that create more problems than solutions.

One of the most important aspects of data quality is **accuracy**. Accurate data correctly measures or records what it claims to represent. In education, inaccurate test scores can place students in the wrong programs. In healthcare, inaccurate medical records can lead to incorrect diagnoses. In business, inaccurate financial data can cause losses or legal trouble. Accuracy is essential because decisions are only as reliable as the information behind them.

Another critical factor is **completeness**. Complete data includes all necessary pieces of information. Missing data can create gaps that lead to false conclusions. For example, if customer feedback is collected from only a small group, it may not reflect the full customer experience. If economic data excludes certain communities, decisions based on that data may unintentionally create inequality. Complete data provides a fuller picture and supports fairer outcomes.

Timeliness also plays a major role in data quality. Data must be current enough to be useful. Outdated data can be dangerous, especially in fast-moving environments. Traffic systems rely on real-time data to manage congestion. Financial systems depend on up-to-date information to manage risk. Even in slower-moving industries, relying on old data can lead to decisions that no longer fit present conditions.

Consistency is another important element. Data should follow the same standards over time. If data is collected using different methods or definitions, comparisons become unreliable. For example, if one department measures success differently than another, combining their data can create confusion. Consistent data allows organizations to track progress, identify trends, and make comparisons with confidence.

Bias is a major challenge affecting data quality. Bias can enter data through the way it is collected, labeled, or interpreted. If data reflects only certain groups or perspectives, decisions based on that data may unfairly advantage or disadvantage others. Recognizing and addressing bias is essential for ethical and responsible decision-making, especially in systems that affect large populations.

Data quality also depends on **verification and validation**. This means checking data for errors, duplicates, and inconsistencies. Organizations often use review processes, automated checks, and audits to ensure data integrity. These steps help prevent small errors from growing into large problems.

Poor data quality does not always come from bad intentions. It often results from rushed collection, unclear standards, limited resources, or outdated systems. However, the consequences can still be serious. This is why organizations invest time and effort into improving how data is collected, stored, and maintained.

For artificial intelligence systems, data quality is especially critical. AI models learn patterns from data. If the data contains errors or bias, the system may learn the wrong lessons and repeat those problems at scale. High-quality data helps AI systems make more reliable and fair decisions.

Understanding data quality helps readers become more thoughtful users and evaluators of information. It encourages them to ask important questions: Is this data accurate? Is anything missing? Is it current? Was it collected fairly? These questions are essential for navigating a data-driven world.

In the next chapter, we will explore **how data is protected**, including security, privacy, and safeguards that help ensure data is used responsibly across every industry.

Why Data Quality Matters

Chapter Summary

This chapter explains why data quality is essential for making good decisions. Simply storing data is not enough—data must be accurate, complete, current, consistent, and fair in order to be useful. Poor-quality data can lead to incorrect conclusions, unfair outcomes, and serious consequences across education, healthcare, business, and government.

The chapter introduces key elements of data quality, including accuracy, completeness, timeliness, consistency, and bias. Accurate data correctly represents reality, while complete data includes all necessary information. Timely data reflects current conditions, and consistent data follows the same standards over time. Bias is highlighted as a major challenge, reminding readers that data reflects human choices and perspectives.

The chapter also explains the importance of verification and validation to catch errors and inconsistencies. It emphasizes that poor data quality is often unintentional but can still cause harm. For artificial intelligence systems, data quality is especially important because AI learns directly from data and can repeat errors at large scale. Overall, the chapter encourages readers to think critically about data and ask thoughtful questions before trusting decisions based on it.

Quiz: Chapter 5

Instructions: Answer the questions below.

1. Why does data quality matter for decision-making?
2. What does it mean for data to be accurate?
3. Give one example of how inaccurate data can cause harm.
4. What is meant by data completeness?
5. Why can missing data lead to unfair outcomes?
6. True or False: Outdated data can still be safe to use in fast-changing systems.
7. What does data consistency help organizations do?
8. How can bias enter data?
9. Why is data quality especially important for AI systems?
10. Name one question a person should ask when evaluating data quality.

Worksheet: Evaluating Data Quality

Part A: Understanding the Concepts

1. Define **data quality** in your own words.
2. List three characteristics of high-quality data.
3. Explain why timeliness is an important part of data quality.

Part B: Real-World Thinking

4. Give one example of data used in school, work, or daily life.
5. What could go wrong if this data is inaccurate or incomplete?
6. How could outdated data affect decisions in this situation?

Part C: Ethics & Responsibility

7. Explain what data bias means using your own words.
8. Why is it important to check data for errors or duplicates?
9. How can poor data quality affect large groups of people?
10. Write one step an organization could take to improve data quality.

Answer Key

Quiz Answers

1. Because decisions are only as reliable as the data behind them.
2. Accurate data correctly represents what actually happened or exists.
3. Incorrect test scores, wrong medical records, or faulty financial reports.
4. Data completeness means all necessary information is included.
5. Because missing data may leave out certain groups or perspectives.
6. **False**
7. It allows reliable comparisons, trend tracking, and progress measurement.
8. Through how data is collected, labeled, or interpreted.
9. Because AI systems learn directly from data and repeat its patterns.
10. Is this data accurate, complete, current, or fair? (answers may vary)

Worksheet Sample Answers

Part A

1. Data quality refers to how accurate, complete, current, and reliable data is.
2. Accuracy, completeness, timeliness, consistency (other answers acceptable).
3. Because outdated data may no longer reflect current conditions.

Part B

4. Grades, attendance records, sales data, or traffic data.
5. Decisions could be unfair, unsafe, or incorrect.
6. It could cause decisions that do not match current needs or conditions.

Part C

7. Data bias occurs when data reflects only certain groups or viewpoints.
8. To prevent small errors from leading to big problems.
9. It can lead to unfair treatment, inequality, or widespread mistakes.
10. Establish clear standards or review processes (answers may vary).

Chapter 6

How Data Is Protected

As data becomes more central to decision-making, protecting it becomes just as important as collecting and storing it. Data protection refers to the practices, systems, and rules used to keep data safe from loss, misuse, unauthorized access, and harm. Across every industry, strong data protection is essential for trust, safety, and long-term stability.

Data protection begins with understanding that not all data carries the same level of risk. Some data is public and intended to be shared, such as published reports or open research. Other data is sensitive and requires strict safeguards. Personal information, financial records, medical histories, and student data must be handled with care because misuse can cause real harm to individuals and organizations.

One of the most important methods of protecting data is **access control**. This means limiting who can see, edit, or use data. In well-designed systems, users are given access only to the data they need to perform their roles. For example, a teacher may access student performance data, but not medical records. A cashier may see transaction details, but not full customer profiles. Limiting access reduces the risk of accidental or intentional misuse.

Another key protection method is **encryption**. Encryption transforms data into a coded form that cannot be read without proper authorization. Even if encrypted data is stolen or intercepted, it remains unusable without the correct keys. Encryption is commonly used when data is stored and when it is transmitted between systems, such as when information is sent over the internet.

Data protection also relies on **authentication systems**. These systems verify that users are who they claim to be before granting access. Passwords, security tokens, biometric scans, and multi-step verification processes all play a role in ensuring that only authorized individuals can access sensitive data. Strong authentication reduces the risk of identity theft and system intrusion.

Regular **backups and recovery plans** are another essential aspect of data protection. Data can be lost due to hardware failure, software errors, natural disasters, or cyberattacks. Backup systems create copies of data that can be restored if the original data is damaged or lost. Recovery planning ensures that organizations can resume operations quickly and minimize disruption.

Protecting data also involves **monitoring and detection**. Many systems track unusual activity, such as repeated login failures or unexpected data transfers. These monitoring tools help identify potential security threats early, allowing organizations to respond before serious damage occurs. Early detection is especially important as cyber threats become more sophisticated.

Laws and regulations play a major role in data protection. Governments establish rules that define how data must be handled, stored, shared, and protected. These laws often require organizations to inform individuals about data collection, limit data usage, and report breaches when they occur. Compliance with these regulations is not optional and reflects society's growing recognition of data rights.

Ethical responsibility is just as important as technical protection. Organizations must decide not only what they can do with data, but what they should do. Responsible data protection includes transparency, respect for privacy, and accountability. Trust is built when people believe their data is handled with care and integrity.

Artificial intelligence systems increase the importance of data protection. AI systems can process large amounts of data quickly, which amplifies both benefits and risks. If protected poorly, AI systems can expose sensitive information or magnify errors at scale. Strong safeguards ensure that intelligence does not come at the cost of privacy or security.

Understanding how data is protected helps readers become more informed and confident participants in a data-driven world. It encourages awareness of rights, responsibilities, and safeguards that exist to protect individuals and communities. Data protection is not a barrier to innovation; it is a foundation that allows innovation to occur responsibly.

In the next chapter, we will explore **how data is used to make decisions**, connecting protection and quality to real-world outcomes across industries.

How Data Is Protected

Chapter Summary

This chapter explains why protecting data is essential in a data-driven world. As data becomes more central to decision-making, it must be kept safe from loss, misuse, and unauthorized access. Data protection includes the systems, rules, and ethical responsibilities that ensure data is handled securely and respectfully.

The chapter describes different methods used to protect data, including access controls, encryption, authentication systems, backups, and monitoring tools. These protections help ensure that only authorized individuals can access sensitive information and that data can be recovered if something goes wrong. The chapter also explains that not all data carries the same level of risk—some data is public, while other data, such as personal, financial, or medical information, requires stronger safeguards.

Legal regulations and ethical responsibility play a key role in data protection. Laws define how organizations must handle data, while ethical decision-making builds trust and accountability. As artificial intelligence systems rely on large amounts of data, strong data protection becomes even more important to prevent harm and protect privacy. Overall, the chapter emphasizes that data protection supports trust, safety, and responsible innovation.

Quiz: Chapter 6

Instructions: Answer the questions below.

1. What is data protection?
2. Why does sensitive data require stronger protection than public data?
3. What is access control, and why is it important?
4. Give one example of how access control limits risk.
5. What does encryption do to data?
6. True or False: Encrypted data can be easily read if it is stolen.
7. Why are authentication systems important?
8. What role do backups play in data protection?
9. How do monitoring systems help protect data?
10. Why is data protection especially important for AI systems?

Worksheet: Understanding Data Protection

Part A: Core Understanding

1. Define **data protection** in your own words.
2. List three methods used to protect stored or transmitted data.
3. Explain why not all data needs the same level of protection.

Part B: Real-World Scenarios

4. Give one example of sensitive data and explain why it must be protected.
5. What could happen if this data were accessed by unauthorized people?
6. How does encryption help reduce harm if data is stolen?

Part C: Ethics & Responsibility

7. Why are laws and regulations important for data protection?
8. Explain the difference between what organizations *can* do with data and what they *should* do.
9. How can poor data protection affect trust in an organization?
10. Write one question you would ask about data protection before using a digital service.

Answer Key

Quiz Answers

1. Data protection refers to the practices and systems used to keep data safe from misuse, loss, or unauthorized access.
2. Because misuse of sensitive data can cause real harm to individuals and organizations.
3. Access control limits who can view or use data to reduce misuse.
4. A teacher accessing grades but not medical records.
5. Encryption turns data into coded information that cannot be read without authorization.
6. **False**
7. They verify user identity before granting access.

8. They allow data to be restored if it is lost or damaged.
9. They detect unusual activity and potential security threats early.
10. Because AI systems process large amounts of data and can amplify risks if data is poorly protected.

Worksheet Sample Answers

Part A

1. Data protection is the process of keeping data safe and secure.
2. Access controls, encryption, authentication, backups, monitoring.
3. Some data is public, while sensitive data can cause harm if misused.

Part B

4. Medical records, financial information, or student data.
5. Identity theft, financial loss, or personal harm.
6. It prevents unauthorized users from understanding the data.

Part C

7. They ensure organizations handle data responsibly and protect individual rights.
8. What they can do may be legal, but what they should do considers ethics and trust.
9. It can reduce confidence and damage relationships with users.
10. How is my data protected and who can access it? (answers may vary)

Chapter 7

How Data Is Used to Make Decisions

Once data is collected, stored, protected, and verified for quality, it becomes a powerful tool for decision-making. Data-driven decision-making means using information—not guesses or assumptions—to guide choices. Across every industry, this approach helps individuals and organizations act with greater clarity, consistency, and confidence.

Data is first used to **describe what is happening**. This is often called understanding the current situation. In schools, data shows attendance patterns, grades, and learning progress. In healthcare, data describes patient conditions and treatment results. In business, data reflects sales, expenses, and customer behavior. Before decisions can be made, decision-makers must clearly see what is occurring.

Next, data is used to **identify patterns and trends**. Patterns emerge when data is examined over time or across groups. For example, a school may notice that certain subjects consistently challenge students. A business may observe that sales increase during specific seasons. A city may detect traffic congestion at predictable times. Recognizing patterns helps decision-makers move beyond isolated events and understand broader behavior.

Data is also used to **compare options**. Decision-making often involves choosing between alternatives. Data allows comparisons based on evidence rather than opinion. For example, an organization may compare the effectiveness of two programs, products, or strategies. By examining outcomes, costs, and impacts, data helps clarify which option is more likely to succeed.

Another important use of data is **prediction**. Historical data can be analyzed to estimate what may happen in the future. Forecasting enrollment, demand, risks, or resource needs helps organizations prepare rather than react. While predictions are never perfect, data-driven forecasts are usually more reliable than intuition alone.

Data also supports **evaluation and improvement**. After a decision is made, data helps measure results. Did the decision achieve its goal? Were there unintended consequences? In education, data shows whether a new teaching approach improved learning. In healthcare, data reveals whether a treatment plan worked. In business, data tracks whether a strategy increased efficiency or revenue. This feedback loop allows continuous improvement.

In many systems, data is processed through **analytical tools and models**. These tools organize and analyze data to highlight relationships and outcomes. Artificial intelligence and machine learning systems use data to detect complex patterns that may not be visible to humans alone. However, these systems still depend on human oversight to interpret results responsibly.

It is important to understand that **data does not make decisions by itself**. Data informs decisions, but people define goals, values, and priorities. A system may show multiple possible outcomes, but humans must choose which path aligns with ethical standards, social responsibility, and long-term goals. Data supports judgment; it does not replace it.

Data-driven decision-making also requires **context and balance**. Numbers alone do not capture human experiences, emotions, or values. Effective decision-makers combine data with professional expertise, community input, and ethical consideration. When data is used without context, it can oversimplify complex situations.

As data-driven systems become more common, the ability to understand and question decisions becomes increasingly important. Readers who understand how data influences decisions are better equipped to participate in discussions, ask informed questions, and hold systems accountable.

This chapter connects the technical foundations of data to real-world impact. Data becomes meaningful only when it is used thoughtfully and responsibly. In the next chapter, we will explore **how different industries apply data-driven decision-making**, beginning with education and expanding across society.

How Data Is Used to Make Decisions

Chapter Summary

This chapter explains how data is used to support decision-making once it has been collected, stored, protected, and verified for quality. Data-driven decision-making means using evidence rather than guesses or assumptions to guide choices. Across many fields, data helps people understand situations clearly and act with greater confidence.

The chapter shows how data is first used to describe what is currently happening. It then explains how data reveals patterns and trends over time, allowing decision-makers to understand behavior rather than isolated events. Data is also used to compare options, helping organizations choose between different strategies or solutions based on evidence.

Another important role of data is prediction. By analyzing historical data, organizations can estimate future needs and risks. Data also supports evaluation by measuring whether decisions achieved their intended goals and identifying areas for improvement. While analytical tools and AI systems can process large amounts of data, human judgment remains essential. Data informs decisions, but people provide values, ethics, and context. The chapter emphasizes that responsible decision-making combines data with experience, human insight, and ethical consideration.

Quiz: Chapter 7

Instructions: Answer the questions below.

1. What does data-driven decision-making mean?
2. Why is data first used to describe what is happening?
3. What is a pattern or trend in data?
4. Give one example of how data can be used to compare options.
5. How does historical data help with prediction?
6. True or False: Data makes decisions without human involvement.
7. Why is evaluation important after a decision is made?
8. How do AI and analytical tools support decision-making?
9. Why is human judgment still necessary when using data?
10. What risk exists when data is used without context?

Worksheet: Using Data to Make Decisions

Part A: Understanding the Process

1. In your own words, explain how data supports decision-making.
2. List three ways data is used before a decision is made.
3. Explain the difference between describing data and predicting outcomes.

Part B: Real-World Application

4. Give one example of a decision made at school, work, or home.
5. What type of data could be used to support this decision?
6. How could data help improve the decision over time?

Part C: Judgment, Ethics, and Balance

7. Why does data not replace human judgment?
8. Give one example of information that data alone cannot fully capture.
9. Why is it important to ask questions about data-driven decisions?
10. Write one question you would ask before accepting a decision based on data.

Answer Key

Quiz Answers

1. Using information and evidence to guide decisions instead of guesses.
2. So decision-makers can clearly understand the current situation.
3. A repeated behavior or trend that appears over time or across groups.
4. Comparing the results or costs of two programs or strategies.
5. It helps estimate what may happen in the future based on past patterns.
6. **False**
7. To measure results and identify improvements or unintended effects.
8. They analyze data and highlight patterns or relationships.
9. Because humans provide values, ethics, and interpretation.
10. It can oversimplify complex situations or lead to poor decisions.

Worksheet Sample Answers

Part A

1. Data helps people make informed choices based on evidence.
2. Describing current conditions, identifying patterns, comparing options.
3. Describing explains what is happening now; predicting estimates what may happen next.

Part B

4. Choosing a class schedule, budgeting money, planning a school event.
5. Attendance records, costs, feedback, or performance data.
6. By measuring results and adjusting decisions based on outcomes.

Part C

7. Because data does not understand values, ethics, or human needs.
8. Emotions, fairness, community impact, or personal experiences.

9. To ensure decisions are fair, accurate, and responsible.
10. What data was used and what might be missing? (answers may vary)

Chapter 8

Data-Driven Decisions in Education

Education is one of the most important areas where data-driven decision-making plays a powerful role. Schools, teachers, administrators, and policymakers rely on data to understand how students learn, where support is needed, and how educational systems can improve over time. When used responsibly, data helps create learning environments that are fair, effective, and responsive to student needs.

In the classroom, data helps teachers understand student progress. Test results, assignments, attendance records, and participation patterns provide insight into how well students are grasping material. This information allows teachers to adjust instruction, offer extra support, or introduce new strategies when students struggle. Rather than relying on assumptions, educators can make informed decisions based on evidence.

Data also supports **early intervention**. Patterns in attendance, behavior, or academic performance can signal when a student may be at risk of falling behind. Identifying these signals early allows schools to provide tutoring, counseling, or additional resources before challenges become more serious. Early intervention is one of the most effective ways data improves educational outcomes.

At the school level, administrators use data to evaluate programs and allocate resources. Enrollment trends help schools plan staffing and classroom space. Performance data helps determine which programs are effective and which may need improvement. Budget decisions are often guided by data that shows where resources will have the greatest impact on student success.

Education data also plays a role beyond individual schools. Districts and education departments analyze data to assess curriculum effectiveness, track graduation rates, and identify achievement gaps. This information helps guide policy decisions and long-term planning. When data is used carefully, it can support equity by highlighting areas where additional support is needed.

Technology has expanded how educational data is collected and used. Digital learning platforms generate data on student engagement, learning pace, and content mastery. These systems can provide real-time feedback to teachers and students, helping personalize learning experiences. However, this increased data collection also raises important questions about privacy and consent, especially for minors.

Protecting student data is a critical responsibility. Educational institutions must ensure that personal information is stored securely and used only for appropriate purposes. Transparency with students and families builds trust and ensures that data supports learning rather than creating risk.

It is important to remember that **data does not define a student**. Data reflects performance at a moment in time, not a person's potential or character. Effective educators use data as a tool, not a label. They combine data with professional judgment, empathy, and understanding of individual circumstances.

When used thoughtfully, data helps education systems move from reactive decisions to proactive planning. It supports continuous improvement and helps schools adapt to changing needs. As education continues to evolve in a data-driven world, understanding how data informs decisions empowers students, educators, and families alike.

In the next chapter, we will explore **how data drives decisions in healthcare**, where accuracy and responsibility can have life-changing consequences.

Data-Driven Decisions in Education

Chapter Summary

This chapter explains how data is used to support decision-making in education. Schools, teachers, administrators, and policymakers rely on data to understand student learning, identify challenges, and improve educational systems. When used responsibly, data helps create learning environments that are fair, effective, and supportive of student growth.

In classrooms, teachers use data such as test results, assignments, attendance, and participation to monitor student progress and adjust instruction. Data also supports early intervention by identifying patterns that may signal when a student needs additional help. Acting early allows schools to provide support before challenges become more serious.

At the school and district levels, data guides program evaluation, resource allocation, and long-term planning. Technology has expanded the collection and use of educational data through digital learning platforms, but this also increases the importance of protecting student privacy. The chapter emphasizes that data does not define a student; it is a tool that must be combined with empathy, professional judgment, and understanding. Used thoughtfully, data helps education systems move from reactive decisions to proactive improvement.

Quiz: Chapter 8

Instructions: Answer the questions below.

1. Why is data important in education?
2. Name two types of data teachers use to understand student progress.
3. What is early intervention, and why is it effective?

4. How do school administrators use data?
5. What role does data play at the district or policy level?
6. True or False: Data should be used to label students permanently.
7. How has technology changed educational data collection?
8. Why is protecting student data especially important?
9. Why must educators combine data with empathy and judgment?
10. How can data help schools move from reactive to proactive planning?

Worksheet: Data Use in Education

Part A: Understanding Educational Data

1. In your own words, explain how data helps teachers support students.
2. List three examples of educational data used in schools.
3. Why is early identification of learning challenges important?

Part B: School & System Decisions

4. Give one example of how a school might use data to improve a program.
5. How can enrollment data help administrators plan for the future?
6. What risks exist if educational data is misunderstood or misused?

Part C: Ethics, Privacy, and Students

7. Why does data not define a student's potential?
8. Give one example of how privacy should be protected in schools.
9. Why is transparency with families important when collecting data?
10. Write one question a student or parent could ask about how school data is used.

Answer Key

Quiz Answers

1. It helps educators understand learning, identify needs, and improve outcomes.
2. Test results, assignments, attendance, participation (any two).
3. Early intervention identifies problems early and provides support before they worsen.
4. To evaluate programs, plan resources, and guide budgeting decisions.
5. To assess performance, track trends, and guide policy decisions.
6. **False**
7. It allows real-time tracking of engagement, progress, and learning pace.
8. Because student data is sensitive and misuse can cause harm.
9. Because data alone cannot capture personal circumstances or potential.
10. By identifying trends early and planning improvements ahead of time.

Worksheet Sample Answers

Part A

1. It shows how students are doing and where support is needed.
2. Grades, attendance, behavior records, test scores.
3. It allows support before students fall further behind.

Part B
4. Improving a reading program based on test results.
5. It helps predict class sizes, staffing, and space needs.
6. It can lead to unfair decisions or misunderstandings.

Part C
7. Because it reflects performance at a moment in time, not ability or character.
8. Limiting access to student records and using secure systems.
9. It builds trust and helps families understand how data supports learning.
10. How is my child's data used and who can access it? (answers may vary)

Chapter 9

Data-Driven Decisions in Healthcare

Healthcare is one of the most critical industries where data-driven decisions have a direct impact on human lives. Doctors, nurses, researchers, administrators, and public health officials rely on data to diagnose illness, plan treatments, improve patient care, and protect communities. In healthcare, accurate and timely data can mean the difference between recovery and serious harm.

At the individual level, patient data forms the foundation of medical care. Medical histories, test results, vital signs, imaging scans, and treatment records help healthcare providers understand a patient's condition. This data allows doctors to identify patterns, track changes over time, and make informed decisions about diagnoses and treatment plans. Without reliable data, healthcare providers would be forced to rely on guesswork rather than evidence.

Data also supports **clinical decision-making**. When a patient presents symptoms, healthcare professionals compare current data with known medical knowledge and past cases. Lab results, imaging data, and monitoring systems provide objective information that guides treatment choices. In emergency situations, fast access to accurate data can be lifesaving.

Healthcare data is essential for **monitoring and prevention**. Data collected from routine checkups, wearable devices, and public health systems helps identify early warning signs of disease. Tracking trends such as rising infection rates or chronic condition patterns allows healthcare systems to respond proactively. Preventive care decisions, such as vaccinations and screenings, are guided by large-scale data analysis.

Medical research depends heavily on data. Researchers analyze clinical trial results, population health data, and treatment outcomes to develop new medications, therapies, and medical procedures. Reliable data helps ensure that treatments are safe and effective before they are widely adopted. Poor-quality or incomplete data can delay progress or lead to incorrect conclusions.

Hospitals and healthcare organizations also use data for **operational decisions**. Staffing levels, equipment availability, appointment scheduling, and supply management are guided by data trends. These decisions help reduce wait times, improve patient experiences, and ensure resources are used efficiently.

Artificial intelligence is increasingly used in healthcare, but it still relies on data as its foundation. AI systems analyze medical images, predict patient risks, and assist in diagnostics by learning from large datasets. However, these systems require high-quality, diverse, and carefully managed data to avoid errors or bias. Human oversight remains essential to ensure AI supports, rather than replaces, medical judgment.

Privacy and protection are especially important in healthcare. Medical data is among the most sensitive types of information. Healthcare providers must follow strict regulations that govern how patient data is collected, stored, shared, and protected. Ethical responsibility is central to maintaining trust between patients and healthcare systems.

It is also important to recognize the limitations of data in healthcare. Data does not capture every aspect of a patient's experience. Emotional well-being, personal circumstances, and individual preferences must be considered alongside clinical data. Effective healthcare decisions balance data with compassion and professional expertise.

Data-driven healthcare continues to evolve as technology advances. From personalized medicine to population health planning, data supports more precise, efficient, and equitable care. Understanding how data influences healthcare decisions helps readers appreciate the complexity and responsibility involved in protecting human health.

In the next chapter, we will explore **how data drives decisions in business and entrepreneurship**, where data influences growth, strategy, and sustainability across industries.

Data-Driven Decisions in Healthcare

Chapter Summary

This chapter explains how data-driven decision-making plays a vital role in healthcare, where decisions directly affect human lives. Healthcare professionals rely on data to diagnose illness, plan treatments, monitor patient health, and improve care outcomes. Accurate and timely data allows providers to move beyond guesswork and make informed, evidence-based decisions.

At the individual level, patient data such as medical histories, test results, vital signs, and imaging scans helps doctors understand conditions and track changes over time. Data also supports clinical decision-making by allowing healthcare providers to compare symptoms and results with known medical knowledge. In emergencies, quick access to reliable data can save lives.

Healthcare data is also essential for prevention, research, and operations. Public health data helps detect disease trends and guide preventive care, while research data supports the development of new treatments and therapies. Hospitals use data to manage staffing, equipment, and resources efficiently. Although artificial intelligence is increasingly used in healthcare, it depends on high-quality data and must always be guided by human oversight. The chapter emphasizes that data must be balanced with compassion, ethics, and professional judgment to support safe and effective healthcare.

Quiz: Chapter 9

Instructions: Answer the questions below.

1. Why is data especially important in healthcare?
2. Name three types of patient data used in medical care.
3. How does data support clinical decision-making?
4. Why is fast access to accurate data critical in emergencies?
5. How does healthcare data support prevention efforts?
6. True or False: Medical research can succeed without reliable data.
7. How do hospitals use data for operational decisions?
8. What role does artificial intelligence play in healthcare decisions?
9. Why is privacy especially important for healthcare data?
10. Why must healthcare decisions balance data with compassion?

Worksheet: Data Use in Healthcare

Part A: Understanding Healthcare Data

1. In your own words, explain how data helps doctors treat patients.
2. List three examples of healthcare data mentioned in the chapter.
3. Why is accurate data better than relying on guesswork in medicine?

Part B: Prevention, Research, and Operations

4. Give one example of how data helps prevent illness.
5. How does data support medical research and innovation?
6. Why do hospitals use data to manage staffing and resources?

Part C: Ethics, AI, and Human Judgment

7. Why does AI in healthcare still require human oversight?

8. What risks exist if healthcare data is incomplete or biased?
9. Why doesn't data capture every aspect of a patient's experience?
10. Write one question a patient might ask about how their medical data is used.

Answer Key

Quiz Answers

1. Because healthcare decisions directly affect human lives and safety.
2. Medical histories, test results, vital signs, imaging scans (any three).
3. It provides objective information that guides diagnosis and treatment.
4. Because delays or errors can be life-threatening.
5. By identifying early warning signs and disease trends.
6. **False**
7. To plan staffing, manage equipment, and improve patient flow.
8. AI analyzes data to assist with diagnostics and risk prediction.
9. Because misuse of medical data can cause serious harm.
10. Because emotional, personal, and ethical factors matter in care.

Worksheet Sample Answers

Part A

1. It helps doctors understand conditions and choose treatments.
2. Lab results, imaging scans, patient histories.
3. Because evidence-based decisions are safer and more reliable.

Part B

4. Tracking infection rates to guide vaccinations or screenings.
5. By analyzing trial results to ensure treatments are safe and effective.
6. To reduce wait times and ensure efficient care delivery.

Part C

7. Because AI cannot replace medical judgment or ethical responsibility.
8. It can lead to incorrect diagnoses or unfair treatment.
9. Because emotions, preferences, and circumstances are not numbers.
10. Who can access my data and how is it protected? (answers may vary)

Chapter 10

Data-Driven Decisions in Business and Entrepreneurship

In business and entrepreneurship, decisions shape success or failure every day. From small family-owned shops to global corporations, organizations rely on data to understand markets, manage operations, serve customers, and plan for the future. Data-driven decision-making helps businesses move beyond guesswork and make choices based on evidence, patterns, and measurable outcomes.

One of the most common ways businesses use data is to understand **customers**. Sales records, purchasing habits, feedback, and engagement data reveal what customers need, prefer, and value. This information helps businesses decide which products to offer, how to price them, and how to improve customer experiences. When businesses understand their customers through data, they can respond more effectively to changing demands.

Data also plays a critical role in **financial decision-making**. Revenue, expenses, cash flow, and profit margins are tracked through financial data. Business owners use this information to budget, forecast growth, manage costs, and assess risk. Accurate financial data supports responsible planning and helps businesses remain sustainable over time.

Operations depend heavily on data as well. Inventory levels, supply chain performance, delivery times, and production output are all guided by data. For example, a business may use data to determine when to reorder supplies, how much inventory to keep on hand, or which suppliers are most reliable. These decisions reduce waste, prevent shortages, and improve efficiency.

Marketing decisions are increasingly data-driven. Businesses analyze data from advertising campaigns, websites, and social media to understand what messages resonate with audiences. Data shows which strategies attract attention, generate sales, or build loyalty. This allows businesses to invest resources more wisely and avoid ineffective approaches.

For entrepreneurs, data is especially valuable because resources are often limited. Startups and small businesses use data to test ideas, measure results, and adjust strategies quickly. Data helps entrepreneurs learn what works without taking unnecessary risks. Even simple data, such as customer responses or sales trends, can guide meaningful decisions.

Data is also used to **evaluate performance**. Key indicators help businesses measure progress toward goals. These indicators may include customer satisfaction, employee productivity, or operational efficiency. By reviewing performance data regularly, businesses can identify strengths, address weaknesses, and improve over time.

Artificial intelligence and automation increasingly support business decisions, but they still rely on data as their foundation. AI systems analyze large datasets to detect trends, predict demand, or optimize processes. However, business leaders remain responsible for interpreting results and ensuring decisions align with values, ethics, and long-term vision.

It is important to recognize that data does not eliminate uncertainty in business. Markets change, customer behavior evolves, and unexpected events occur. Data provides guidance, not guarantees. Successful businesses combine data insights with experience, creativity, and strategic thinking.

Understanding how data drives business decisions empowers readers to become smarter consumers, more informed employees, and more confident entrepreneurs. Data helps businesses grow responsibly, adapt to change, and contribute positively to the economy.

In the next chapter, we will explore **data-driven decisions in government and public services**, where data influences policies, infrastructure, and community well-being.

Data-Driven Decisions in Business and Entrepreneurship

Chapter Summary

This chapter explains how data-driven decision-making shapes business and entrepreneurship at every level, from small family-owned businesses to global corporations. Businesses rely on data to understand customers, manage finances, improve operations, and plan for growth. Using data allows organizations to make informed decisions instead of relying on guesswork.

Customer data helps businesses understand preferences, purchasing behavior, and feedback, allowing them to improve products and services. Financial data supports budgeting, forecasting, and risk management, helping businesses remain sustainable. Operational data guides inventory management, supply chains, and efficiency, reducing waste and improving reliability.

Marketing decisions are increasingly based on data from advertising, websites, and social media. For entrepreneurs, data is especially valuable because it allows ideas to be tested quickly and adjusted without unnecessary risk. Performance data helps businesses evaluate progress and improve over time. While artificial intelligence supports analysis, business leaders remain responsible for interpreting results and aligning decisions with ethics, values, and long-term goals. Data provides guidance—not guarantees—and works best when combined with experience and creativity.

Quiz: Chapter 10

Instructions: Answer the questions below.

1. Why is data important in business decision-making?
2. Name two ways businesses use customer data.
3. What types of financial data help businesses plan responsibly?
4. How does data support operational decisions?
5. Give one example of a data-driven marketing decision.
6. True or False: Entrepreneurs only need large datasets to make decisions.
7. What is performance data used for?
8. How does artificial intelligence support business decisions?
9. Why does data not eliminate uncertainty in business?
10. How does understanding data-driven business decisions benefit individuals?

Worksheet: Data Use in Business & Entrepreneurship

Part A: Core Understanding

1. In your own words, explain what data-driven decision-making means in business.
2. List three types of business data discussed in the chapter.
3. Why is customer data valuable to businesses?

Part B: Real-World Business Decisions

4. Give an example of a business decision that could be improved using data.
5. What data would be needed to support that decision?
6. How could reviewing data regularly help a business grow?

Part C: Judgment, Risk, and Ethics

7. Why must business leaders still use judgment even when data is available?
8. What risks exist if data is misunderstood or ignored?
9. Why is data especially useful for entrepreneurs with limited resources?
10. Write one question a business owner might ask before acting on data.

Answer Key

Quiz Answers

1. It helps businesses make informed choices based on evidence.
2. Understanding preferences, improving products, setting prices.
3. Revenue, expenses, cash flow, profit margins.
4. By guiding inventory, supply chains, and efficiency.
5. Choosing which advertising campaign to invest in.
6. **False**
7. To measure progress, identify strengths, and improve performance.
8. By analyzing large datasets to detect trends and predict outcomes.
9. Because markets and customer behavior can change unexpectedly.
10. It helps people become smarter consumers and confident entrepreneurs.

Worksheet Sample Answers

Part A

1. Using data to guide business choices instead of guessing.
2. Customer data, financial data, operational data.
3. It helps businesses understand needs and improve experiences.

Part B
4. Deciding how much inventory to order.
5. Sales history, customer demand, delivery times.
6. It helps identify what is working and what needs improvement.

Part C
7. Because data does not account for values, ethics, or creativity.
8. Poor decisions, wasted resources, or lost customers.
9. It allows testing ideas and adjusting quickly with less risk.
10. What does the data show, and what might be missing? (answers may vary)

Chapter 11

Data-Driven Decisions in Government and Public Services

Government and public service organizations make decisions that affect entire communities, cities, and nations. These decisions influence transportation systems, public safety, education funding, healthcare access, housing, and environmental protection. Data plays a central role in helping governments understand public needs, allocate resources, and plan for the future responsibly.

Public agencies use data to understand **population trends**. Census information, demographic data, and economic indicators help governments track changes in population size, age distribution, employment, and housing needs. This data supports decisions about where to build schools, hospitals, roads, and public facilities. Without reliable data, long-term planning would be based on assumptions rather than evidence.

Data is essential for **public safety and emergency response**. Law enforcement agencies analyze crime data to identify patterns and deploy resources more effectively. Fire departments and emergency services use response-time data to improve coverage and readiness. During natural disasters or public health emergencies, real-time data helps coordinate responses, allocate aid, and protect lives.

Transportation and infrastructure decisions are heavily data-driven. Traffic flow data, public transit usage, and road condition reports help cities manage congestion, plan maintenance, and design safer transportation systems. Data allows governments to identify problem areas and prioritize improvements that benefit the greatest number of people.

Public health agencies rely on data to monitor disease outbreaks, vaccination rates, and health trends. This information supports decisions about prevention programs, healthcare funding, and emergency interventions. During health crises, accurate data enables timely responses that can reduce harm and save lives.

Governments also use data to evaluate **program effectiveness**. Social programs, education initiatives, and economic development efforts are assessed using outcome data. By analyzing results, governments can determine which programs are working and which need adjustment or replacement. This helps ensure public funds are used responsibly and transparently.

Data supports accountability and transparency in public services. When governments share data openly, citizens gain insight into how decisions are made and how resources are spent. Open data initiatives allow researchers, journalists, and community members to examine public information and contribute to informed discussions.

However, data use in government also raises important ethical considerations. Governments must balance data-driven decision-making with privacy rights, fairness, and public trust. Sensitive data must be protected, and decisions must avoid reinforcing bias or discrimination. Responsible data governance is essential to maintaining confidence in public institutions.

Technology and artificial intelligence are expanding how governments use data, from smart city systems to automated services. These tools can improve efficiency and responsiveness, but they also require careful oversight to ensure decisions remain human-centered and accountable.

Understanding how data influences government decisions helps readers become more informed citizens. It encourages engagement, critical thinking, and participation in civic life. Data-driven governance, when practiced responsibly, strengthens communities and supports democratic decision-making.

In the next chapter, we will explore **how data influences everyday life**, showing how data-driven decisions affect individuals and families in ways that are often unseen but deeply impactful.

Data-Driven Decisions in Government and Public Services

Chapter Summary

This chapter explains how data-driven decision-making is used in government and public services to support communities, cities, and nations. Governments rely on data to understand population needs, allocate resources fairly, and plan for the future. Decisions about transportation, public safety, healthcare, education, housing, and environmental protection are guided by evidence collected through public data systems.

Population and demographic data help governments plan infrastructure such as schools, hospitals, and roads. Public safety agencies use data to improve emergency response and protect communities. Transportation and infrastructure decisions depend on traffic patterns, usage data, and maintenance reports. Public health agencies rely on data to monitor disease trends, guide prevention efforts, and respond to emergencies.

The chapter also highlights how governments use data to evaluate programs, ensure accountability, and promote transparency through open data initiatives. At the same time, ethical responsibilities remain central. Governments must protect privacy, avoid bias, and maintain public trust. As technology and AI expand government data use, human oversight and responsible governance remain essential. Understanding data-driven government decisions helps readers become informed, engaged citizens who can participate thoughtfully in civic life.

Quiz: Chapter 11

Instructions: Answer the questions below.

1. Why is data important for government and public service decisions?
2. Name two types of population data used by governments.
3. How does data support public safety and emergency response?
4. Give one example of how data influences transportation decisions.
5. How do public health agencies use data?
6. True or False: Governments should keep all data private from the public.
7. What role does data play in evaluating government programs?
8. Why is transparency important in data-driven governance?
9. What ethical concerns must governments consider when using data?
10. How does understanding government data use benefit citizens?

Worksheet: Data Use in Government & Public Services

Part A: Understanding Government Data

1. In your own words, explain how data helps governments serve communities.
2. List three areas of public service that rely on data.
3. Why is population data important for long-term planning?

Part B: Public Safety, Health, and Infrastructure

4. Give one example of how data helps during emergencies.
5. How can traffic or transportation data improve daily life in a city?
6. Why is accurate data critical during public health crises?

Part C: Ethics, Transparency, and Citizenship

7. Why must governments protect sensitive data?
8. How can open data increase trust between governments and citizens?
9. What risks exist if government data reinforces bias or inequality?
10. Write one question a citizen could ask about a data-driven government decision.

Answer Key

Quiz Answers

1. It helps governments understand needs, allocate resources, and plan responsibly.
2. Census data, demographic data, economic indicators.
3. By identifying patterns and improving response times.
4. Managing traffic congestion or planning road maintenance.
5. By tracking disease trends, vaccination rates, and health outcomes.
6. **False**
7. It helps determine whether programs are effective or need changes.
8. It allows citizens to understand decisions and hold institutions accountable.
9. Privacy, fairness, bias prevention, and public trust.
10. It encourages informed participation and civic engagement.

Worksheet Sample Answers

Part A

1. Data helps governments make informed decisions that meet public needs.
2. Public safety, healthcare, transportation, education.
3. It helps plan services and infrastructure for changing populations.

Part B
4. Coordinating disaster response using real-time data.
5. It reduces congestion and improves safety.
6. Because delays or errors can increase harm.

Part C
7. To prevent misuse and protect individual rights.
8. By showing how decisions are made and funds are used.
9. It can lead to unfair policies or unequal treatment.
10. What data was used and whose voices may be missing? (answers may vary)

Chapter 12

Data-Driven Decisions in Everyday Life

Data-driven decisions are not limited to large institutions, governments, or corporations. They affect everyday life in ways that many people do not immediately notice. From the moment individuals wake up to the moment they go to sleep, data quietly influences choices, recommendations, and automated actions that shape daily experiences.

In the home, data powers many modern conveniences. Smart thermostats use temperature data and usage patterns to adjust heating and cooling. Home security systems rely on sensor data to detect movement and alert homeowners. Even household appliances can use data to improve energy efficiency and performance. These systems make decisions automatically, based on data collected over time.

Personal devices generate large amounts of data. Smartphones track location, app usage, communication patterns, and preferences. This data helps devices provide navigation, reminders, personalized content, and accessibility features. While these tools offer convenience, they also highlight the importance of understanding what data is collected and how it is used.

Shopping and consumer experiences are heavily influenced by data. Online stores analyze browsing history, purchase patterns, and reviews to recommend products. Pricing, promotions, and inventory decisions are often based on aggregated consumer data. These systems aim to improve convenience and relevance, but they also shape what people see and how choices are presented.

Entertainment and media platforms rely on data to personalize experiences. Streaming services use viewing history to suggest movies or music. Social media platforms analyze engagement data to determine which content appears in feeds. These data-driven decisions influence attention, habits, and even opinions, making awareness and balance especially important.

Data also plays a role in transportation and mobility. Navigation apps use traffic data, road conditions, and travel patterns to suggest routes. Ride-sharing services use data to match drivers and passengers efficiently. Public transportation systems rely on usage data to adjust schedules and improve service.

Health and wellness decisions are increasingly supported by personal data. Wearable devices track steps, heart rate, sleep patterns, and activity levels. This data helps individuals set goals, monitor progress, and make healthier choices. When shared with healthcare providers, personal data can also support preventive care and early intervention.

Financial decisions in everyday life are influenced by data as well. Budgeting apps analyze spending patterns. Banks use transaction data to detect fraud and manage risk. Credit decisions often rely on financial histories and behavioral data. These systems can provide security and convenience, but they also require transparency and fairness.

It is important to recognize that data-driven systems do not remove personal responsibility. People still make choices, but those choices are shaped by information presented to them. Understanding how data influences recommendations, defaults, and automated decisions empowers individuals to make more informed and intentional choices.

Everyday data use also raises questions about privacy and control. Individuals should be aware of what data they share, who has access to it, and how it is protected. Digital literacy includes understanding rights, settings, and options that allow people to manage their data responsibly.

By recognizing how data-driven decisions appear in daily life, readers gain a clearer understanding of data's reach and impact. Data is not distant or abstract; it is woven into routine experiences. Awareness is the first step toward using data-driven systems wisely and maintaining balance between convenience and control.

In the next chapter, we will explore **ethical responsibility in data use**, examining why trust, fairness, and accountability matter as data continues to shape decisions across every industry.

Data-Driven Decisions in Everyday Life

Chapter Summary

This chapter explains how data-driven decisions influence everyday life, often in ways people do not immediately notice. From home technologies to smartphones, shopping, entertainment, transportation, health, and finances, data quietly shapes daily choices and automated actions. These systems rely on patterns collected over time to improve convenience, efficiency, and personalization.

In homes, smart devices use data to manage energy use and security. Personal devices such as smartphones collect data to provide navigation, reminders, and accessibility features. Shopping platforms and entertainment services analyze user behavior to recommend products, movies, music, or content. Transportation apps use traffic and location data to improve travel efficiency, while wearable devices support health and wellness goals through personal data tracking.

The chapter emphasizes that data-driven systems do not replace personal responsibility. Instead, they influence how options are presented and which choices are encouraged. Understanding how data affects recommendations, defaults, and automation helps individuals make more intentional decisions. The chapter also highlights the importance of privacy awareness and data control. By recognizing how data appears in everyday life, readers gain the awareness needed to balance convenience with responsibility and informed choice.

Quiz: Chapter 12

Instructions: Answer the questions below.

1. Why are data-driven decisions often unnoticed in everyday life?
2. Name two examples of how data is used in the home.
3. What types of data do smartphones commonly collect?
4. How does data influence shopping and consumer experiences?
5. How do entertainment platforms use data to personalize content?
6. True or False: Data-driven systems remove personal responsibility.
7. How does data support transportation and mobility decisions?
8. Give one example of how personal data supports health or wellness.
9. Why is privacy awareness important in everyday data use?
10. How does understanding data-driven decisions empower individuals?

Worksheet: Data in Everyday Life

Part A: Recognizing Everyday Data Use

1. In your own words, explain how data affects daily life.
2. List three everyday activities influenced by data.
3. Why do data-driven systems aim to personalize experiences?

Part B: Choices, Influence, and Responsibility

4. Give one example of a recommendation you receive from a digital system.
5. How might data shape the choices presented to you?
6. Why is it important to question automated suggestions?

Part C: Privacy and Control

7. What types of personal data do people commonly share without thinking about it?
8. Why should individuals understand who has access to their data?
9. How can managing privacy settings help protect personal data?
10. Write one question you would ask before sharing personal data online.

Answer Key

Quiz Answers

1. Because data-driven systems operate quietly in the background.
2. Smart thermostats, security systems, energy-efficient appliances.
3. Location, app usage, communication patterns, preferences.
4. By recommending products, setting prices, and shaping promotions.
5. By analyzing viewing or listening history to suggest content.
6. **False**
7. By optimizing routes, matching services, and improving schedules.
8. Tracking steps, heart rate, sleep, or activity levels.
9. Because personal data can affect privacy, security, and control.
10. It helps people make informed and intentional choices.

Worksheet Sample Answers

Part A

1. Data influences recommendations, automation, and daily choices.
2. Shopping, navigation, entertainment, health tracking.
3. To make services more relevant and convenient.

Part B
4. Movie recommendations, product suggestions, navigation routes.
5. It highlights certain options while hiding others.
6. Because automated choices may not reflect personal values or needs.

Part C
7. Location data, browsing history, app usage.
8. To understand how data may be used or shared.
9. They limit access and reduce misuse.
10. Why is this data needed and how will it be protected? (answers may vary)

Chapter 13

Ethical Responsibility in Data Use

As data becomes more powerful and influential, ethical responsibility becomes essential. Ethical data use means handling data in ways that are fair, transparent, respectful, and accountable. Across every industry, decisions driven by data affect real people, and those impacts create a responsibility to use data wisely and humanely.

Ethical responsibility begins with **respect for individuals**. Data often represents people's lives, behaviors, health, education, finances, and personal choices. Treating data ethically means recognizing that behind every data point is a human being. Decisions based on data can open opportunities, deny access, or shape outcomes, making fairness and care essential.

One core ethical principle is **consent**. Individuals should understand what data is being collected, why it is being collected, and how it will be used. Ethical systems prioritize clarity and honesty, avoiding hidden data practices or misleading agreements. When people are informed and empowered, trust grows between individuals and organizations.

Privacy is another foundational concern. Ethical data use limits access to sensitive information and protects it from misuse. Organizations must ensure that personal data is not exposed, exploited, or shared without justification. Privacy protection is not just a legal obligation; it is a moral one that preserves dignity and autonomy.

Bias is a major ethical challenge in data-driven systems. Data can reflect historical inequalities, incomplete perspectives, or unbalanced representation. When biased data is used to make decisions, those biases can be reinforced or amplified. Ethical responsibility requires identifying, questioning, and addressing bias to ensure decisions do not unfairly harm individuals or groups.

Transparency plays a critical role in ethical data use. People should be able to understand how decisions are made, especially when data-driven systems affect important outcomes such as education placement, healthcare access, employment, or financial opportunities. Transparency allows individuals to question decisions and seek explanations, promoting accountability.

Accountability means that organizations remain responsible for the outcomes of data-driven decisions. Even when automated systems or artificial intelligence are involved, responsibility does not disappear. Humans design, deploy, and oversee these systems, and they must answer for their impacts. Ethical organizations establish oversight processes to review decisions and correct mistakes.

Ethical data use also involves **purpose limitation**. Data collected for one reason should not be used for unrelated purposes without careful consideration and consent. Using data beyond its original intent can erode trust and create harm. Responsible systems clearly define how data will be used and avoid unnecessary expansion of data usage.

Education and awareness are key to ethical responsibility. Decision-makers must understand the implications of data use, and individuals must be informed about their rights and choices. Ethical data cultures are built through training, discussion, and shared values, not just rules and policies.

As artificial intelligence systems grow more advanced, ethical responsibility becomes even more important. AI can process data at a scale and speed beyond human capability, increasing both benefits and risks. Ethical frameworks ensure that technological progress aligns with human values and societal well-being.

Ethical data use is not a barrier to innovation. Instead, it supports sustainable progress by building trust and long-term success. Systems that respect ethics are more likely to be accepted, supported, and effective over time.

This chapter emphasizes a central truth: **how data is used matters as much as what data is used**. Ethical responsibility ensures that data-driven decisions serve people, not just systems.

In the final chapter, we will look ahead to **the future of data-driven decision-making**, exploring how data literacy and responsible practices will shape the next generation.

Ethical Responsibility in Data Use

Chapter Summary

This chapter explains why ethical responsibility is essential as data becomes more powerful and influential in decision-making. Ethical data use means handling data fairly, transparently, respectfully, and with accountability. Because data often represents real people and their lives, decisions based on data can create opportunities or cause harm, making ethical care essential.

The chapter highlights several core ethical principles. Consent ensures individuals understand what data is collected and how it is used. Privacy protects sensitive information and preserves dignity. Bias presents a major challenge, as data can reflect historical inequalities that may be reinforced if not addressed. Transparency allows people to understand and question how decisions are made, while accountability ensures that organizations remain responsible for outcomes—even when automation or AI is involved.

Ethical responsibility also includes purpose limitation, meaning data should only be used for clearly defined and appropriate reasons. Education and awareness help build ethical data cultures by ensuring that both decision-makers and individuals understand rights, responsibilities, and impacts. As AI systems expand, ethical frameworks ensure innovation aligns with human values. The chapter emphasizes that ethical data use is not a barrier to progress, but a foundation for trust, sustainability, and long-term success.

Quiz: Chapter 13

Instructions: Answer the questions below.

1. What does ethical data use mean?
2. Why is it important to remember that data represents real people?
3. What is consent in the context of data collection?
4. Why is privacy both a legal and moral responsibility?
5. How can bias enter data-driven systems?
6. True or False: Transparency allows people to question data-driven decisions.
7. What does accountability mean when AI systems are used?
8. Explain the idea of purpose limitation.
9. Why are education and awareness important for ethical data use?
10. How does ethical responsibility support long-term innovation?

Worksheet: Ethical Responsibility in Data Use

Part A: Core Ethical Principles

1. In your own words, explain what ethical responsibility in data use means.
2. List four ethical principles discussed in the chapter.
3. Why is consent important for building trust?

Part B: Bias, Transparency, and Accountability

4. Give one example of how bias could affect a data-driven decision.
5. Why is transparency important when decisions affect education, healthcare, or jobs?
6. Who is responsible when a data-driven system causes harm?

Part C: Purpose, Awareness, and the Future

7. What does it mean to use data only for its intended purpose?
8. Why should individuals understand their data rights and choices?
9. How does ethical data use protect both people and organizations?
10. Write one question you would ask to evaluate whether a data practice is ethical.

Answer Key

Quiz Answers

1. Using data fairly, transparently, responsibly, and with respect for people.
2. Because decisions based on data can directly affect lives and opportunities.
3. When individuals are informed about data collection and agree to it.
4. Because misuse of personal data can harm dignity, autonomy, and trust.
5. Through incomplete data, historical inequality, or unbalanced representation.
6. **True**
7. Humans remain responsible for the system's design and outcomes.
8. Using data only for the reason it was originally collected.
9. They help people understand impacts, rights, and responsibilities.
10. By building trust and ensuring systems are accepted and sustainable.

Worksheet Sample Answers

Part A

1. It means using data in ways that respect people and avoid harm.
2. Consent, privacy, fairness, transparency, accountability.
3. Because people feel respected and informed about how data is used.

Part B
4. Biased hiring data leading to unfair job decisions.
5. Because people deserve explanations for decisions that affect their lives.
6. The organization and humans overseeing the system.

Part C
7. Not using data for unrelated purposes without permission.
8. So individuals can protect themselves and make informed choices.
9. It prevents harm and builds long-term trust.
10. Who benefits from this data use, and who might be harmed? (answers may vary)

Chapter 14

The Future of Data-Driven Decisions

As society moves deeper into the digital age, data-driven decision-making will continue to shape how the world operates. The future of education, healthcare, business, government, and everyday life will depend not only on the availability of data, but on how responsibly and intelligently it is used. Understanding this future begins with recognizing that data is no longer optional—it is foundational.

In the years ahead, data will become more **integrated, continuous, and interconnected**. Systems will rely on real-time data streams rather than static records. Decisions that once took weeks or months will increasingly happen in seconds. Transportation systems will adjust automatically, healthcare monitoring will become more predictive, and businesses will respond instantly to changing conditions. This speed brings opportunity, but it also increases responsibility.

Artificial intelligence will play a growing role in data-driven decisions, but AI will not replace human judgment. Instead, AI will act as a tool that analyzes large volumes of data and highlights patterns, risks, or opportunities. Humans will remain responsible for defining goals, values, and boundaries. The future will depend on strong partnerships between human decision-makers and intelligent systems.

Data literacy will be one of the most important skills of the next generation. Just as reading and math became essential in earlier eras, understanding data will become a basic requirement for participation in society. Students, workers, parents, and leaders will need to understand how data is collected, interpreted, and applied. Data literacy empowers people to question decisions, recognize bias, and protect their rights.

The future will also bring increased attention to **ethics and governance**. As data-driven systems grow more powerful, societies will demand clearer rules, stronger protections, and greater transparency. Trust will become a defining factor in whether systems are accepted or rejected. Organizations that prioritize ethical data practices will earn confidence and long-term success.

Data will continue to blur the boundaries between industries. Education data will influence workforce planning. Healthcare data will shape public policy. Environmental data will guide business and infrastructure decisions. This interconnectedness will require collaboration across fields and shared responsibility for outcomes.

At the same time, individuals will play a more active role in managing their own data. Awareness of privacy, consent, and control will increase. People will expect to understand how their data is used and to have a voice in how systems affect their lives. Empowered individuals strengthen democratic and equitable decision-making.

The future of data-driven decisions is not predetermined. It will be shaped by choices made today—choices about education, ethics, access, and accountability. Data itself is neutral, but its use reflects human values. Whether data-driven systems create opportunity or inequality depends on how thoughtfully they are designed and governed.

This book has shown that data is not just a technical concept. It is a practical force that influences decisions in every industry and in everyday life. By understanding data, readers gain the ability to engage with modern systems confidently and responsibly.

The future belongs to those who understand not only **how data works**, but **why it matters**. Data-driven decisions, guided by human judgment and ethical responsibility, have the power to support progress, fairness, and well-being across society.

The Future of Data-Driven Decisions

Chapter Summary

This chapter explores how data-driven decision-making will shape the future of society. As the digital age continues to expand, data will become more integrated, real-time, and interconnected across all industries. Decisions that once took long periods of time will increasingly happen quickly, creating both powerful opportunities and greater responsibility.

Artificial intelligence will play a growing role in analyzing data, but it will not replace human judgment. Instead, AI will support people by identifying patterns, risks, and opportunities, while humans remain responsible for values, goals, and ethical boundaries. The chapter emphasizes that strong collaboration between humans and intelligent systems will define successful decision-making in the future.

Data literacy emerges as a critical skill for the next generation. Understanding how data is collected, interpreted, and used empowers individuals to question decisions, recognize bias, and protect their rights. Ethical responsibility, transparency, and governance will become increasingly important as systems grow more powerful. The chapter concludes by reinforcing that data itself is neutral, but how it is used reflects human values. The future of data-driven decisions will be shaped by the choices people make today.

Quiz: Chapter 14

Instructions: Answer the questions below.

1. Why is data considered foundational in the future?
2. How will real-time data change decision-making speed?
3. What role will artificial intelligence play in future data-driven decisions?
4. True or False: AI will replace human judgment in decision-making.
5. Why is data literacy important for future generations?
6. What does ethical governance mean in the context of data use?
7. How will data blur boundaries between industries?
8. Why is trust important for data-driven systems?
9. What role will individuals play in managing their own data?
10. What determines whether data-driven systems create opportunity or inequality?

Worksheet: Preparing for the Future of Data

Part A: Understanding the Future

1. In your own words, describe how data-driven decisions will change in the future.
2. List three areas of life that will be influenced by future data-driven systems.
3. Why does faster decision-making increase responsibility?

Part B: Human Judgment, AI, and Literacy

4. Explain why AI is a tool rather than a replacement for humans.
5. What does it mean to be data literate?
6. How can data literacy help people recognize bias or unfairness?

Part C: Ethics, Choice, and Responsibility

7. Why is ethical responsibility essential in future data use?
8. How can individuals protect and manage their own data?
9. Why is the future of data-driven decisions not predetermined?
10. Write one action you can take to become a more responsible data user.

Answer Key

Quiz Answers

1. Because data underlies decisions in every industry and daily life.
2. Decisions will happen faster, often in seconds rather than weeks.
3. AI will analyze data and highlight patterns and risks.
4. **False**
5. It helps people understand, question, and protect their rights.
6. Establishing rules, protections, and accountability for data use.
7. By allowing data from one field to influence decisions in another.
8. Without trust, systems will not be accepted or supported.
9. Individuals will have more awareness, control, and voice over data use.
10. Human choices about ethics, design, and governance.

Worksheet Sample Answers

Part A

1. Data will be used faster and across more systems to guide decisions.
2. Education, healthcare, transportation, business, government.
3. Because mistakes can spread quickly and affect many people.

Part B

4. AI processes data, but humans decide values and goals.
5. Understanding how data is collected, used, and interpreted.
6. It helps people question where data comes from and how it's used.

Part C

7. Because data affects real people and societal outcomes.
8. By understanding privacy settings, consent, and data rights.
9. Because human decisions today shape how systems are built.
10. Learning about data privacy or questioning automated decisions. (answers may vary)

Chapter 15

Data Centers: Where Data Lives and Works

Behind every digital service, intelligent system, and data-driven decision is a physical place where data is stored, processed, and protected. These places are called **data centers**. Although most people never see them, data centers are among the most important pieces of infrastructure in the modern world.

A data center is a specialized facility designed to house computer systems that store, process, and manage large amounts of data. Inside a data center are powerful servers, networking equipment, storage systems, and security technologies working together continuously. These systems operate day and night to ensure that data is available when needed.

Data centers exist because digital information must live somewhere physical. Even though people often talk about "the cloud," the cloud is not an abstract space. It is made up of data centers located around the world. When someone sends an email, streams a video, accesses a school platform, or uses an AI system, the data involved is being handled inside one or more data centers.

The primary role of a data center is **data storage and processing**. Data centers store information such as documents, images, videos, databases, and application data. They also process data by running software applications, analyzing information, and supporting artificial intelligence systems. This processing allows systems to respond quickly to requests and make real-time decisions.

Reliability is a key requirement of data centers. Because so many services depend on them, data centers are designed to minimize downtime. They use backup power supplies, generators, and redundant systems to continue operating even during power outages or emergencies. This reliability ensures that critical services, such as healthcare systems, financial transactions, and public infrastructure, remain available.

Cooling and energy management are essential parts of data center design. Servers generate significant heat while processing data. Data centers use advanced cooling systems to maintain safe operating temperatures and prevent equipment damage. Energy efficiency has become increasingly important as data usage grows, leading to innovations in sustainable power and cooling technologies.

Security is another core function of data centers. Physical security measures include controlled access, surveillance, and monitoring to prevent unauthorized entry. Digital security measures protect data from cyber threats such as hacking or data breaches. Together, these protections help ensure that sensitive information remains safe and trustworthy.

Data centers vary in size and purpose. Some are small facilities serving a single organization, such as a school district or hospital system. Others are massive complexes operated by global technology companies, supporting millions of users simultaneously. Regardless of size, all data centers play a role in keeping data accessible and functional.

Artificial intelligence systems depend heavily on data centers. Training AI models requires immense computing power and access to large datasets, which data centers provide. Even after training, AI systems rely on data centers to run models, process requests, and deliver results to users. As AI adoption increases, data centers become even more central to decision-making systems.

Data centers also support **data sharing and connectivity**. High-speed networks connect data centers to users, devices, and other data centers. This connectivity allows data to move quickly and securely across regions and industries. Global collaboration, cloud computing, and real-time services all rely on these connections.

Despite their importance, data centers raise important considerations. Energy use, environmental impact, and location decisions must be managed responsibly. Communities and organizations increasingly consider sustainability, efficiency, and transparency when building and operating data centers.

Understanding data centers helps readers see the physical reality behind digital systems. Data-driven decisions do not happen magically or invisibly. They depend on real infrastructure, real energy, and real human planning. Data centers are the engines that keep the digital world running.

As data continues to grow in importance, data centers will remain foundational to every industry. They are not just storage spaces; they are active environments where data lives, moves, and becomes actionable information.

Chapter Summary

This chapter explains what data centers are and why they are essential to the modern digital world. Although most people interact with digital services through screens, the data behind those services is stored and processed in physical facilities called data centers. These centers house servers, storage systems, networking equipment, and security technologies that operate continuously to keep data accessible and functional.

The chapter clarifies that "the cloud" is not abstract—it is made up of real data centers located around the world. Data centers store and process information for everyday activities such as emailing, streaming, learning platforms, and artificial intelligence systems. Reliability is a core requirement, so data centers use backup power, redundancy, and careful design to prevent downtime.

Cooling, energy management, and security are critical aspects of data center operations. As AI systems grow, data centers provide the computing power needed to train and run models. The chapter also highlights important considerations such as sustainability, energy use, and environmental impact. Overall, data centers are presented as active, physical environments that make data-driven decisions possible across every industry.

Quiz: Chapter 15

Instructions: Answer the questions below.

1. What is a data center?
2. Why do data centers exist if data is digital?
3. What does the term "cloud" actually refer to?
4. Name two types of systems found inside a data center.
5. Why is reliability critical for data centers?
6. True or False: Data centers only store data and do not process it.
7. Why are cooling systems important in data centers?
8. How do data centers protect data from physical threats?
9. What role do data centers play in artificial intelligence systems?
10. Why is sustainability an important consideration for data centers?

Worksheet: Understanding Data Centers

Part A: Core Concepts

1. In your own words, explain what a data center does.
2. List three services or activities that rely on data centers.
3. Why is it important to understand that data lives in physical places?

Part B: Reliability, Security, and Energy

4. How do backup power systems help data centers remain reliable?
5. Why must data centers manage heat and energy carefully?
6. What is one example of a physical security measure used in data centers?

Part C: Data Centers and the Future

7. How do data centers support AI training and use?
8. Why do data centers need fast network connections?
9. What environmental concerns are associated with data centers?
10. Write one question you would ask before building a new data center in a community.

Answer Key

Quiz Answers

1. A specialized facility that stores, processes, and manages data.
2. Because digital data must be stored and processed on physical machines.
3. A network of data centers located around the world.
4. Servers, storage systems, networking equipment.
5. Because many critical services depend on them operating continuously.
6. **False**
7. To prevent overheating and equipment damage.
8. Controlled access, surveillance, and monitoring.
9. They provide computing power to train and run AI models.
10. Because data centers use large amounts of energy and affect the environment.

Worksheet Sample Answers

Part A

1. It stores and processes data so digital services can work.
2. Streaming video, email, online learning, AI tools.
3. It helps people understand the real infrastructure behind digital systems.

Part B

4. They keep systems running during power outages.
5. To maintain safe temperatures and reduce energy waste.
6. Locked access points, cameras, security staff.

Part C

7. By supplying computing power and access to large datasets.
8. To move data quickly between users, systems, and locations.
9. Energy consumption and environmental impact.
10. How will energy use and environmental impact be managed? (answers may vary)

Chapter 16

Cloud Computing and Data Centers: How They Work Together

Many people hear the terms *cloud computing* and *data centers* used interchangeably, but they are not the same thing. Understanding the difference between them—and how they work together—helps clarify how modern digital systems operate and how data-driven decisions happen at scale.

A **data center** is a physical facility. It is a real building filled with servers, storage systems, networking equipment, power supplies, and cooling systems. Data centers provide the hardware and infrastructure that make digital services possible. They are where data is physically stored and processed.

Cloud computing, on the other hand, is a service model. It describes how computing resources—such as storage, processing power, and software—are delivered to users over the internet. When people use cloud services, they are not accessing a single computer or server. They are accessing resources that are managed across many data centers.

In simple terms, **data centers are the foundation**, and **cloud computing is the way those resources are delivered and used**.

Cloud computing allows organizations and individuals to access data and computing power without owning or managing physical servers themselves. Instead of buying hardware, installing software, and maintaining systems, users rent access to computing resources as needed. This flexibility has transformed how schools, businesses, governments, and startups operate.

There are several reasons cloud computing became so widely adopted. One reason is **scalability**. Cloud systems can expand or shrink quickly based on demand. For example, a school district can increase online learning capacity during testing periods and reduce it afterward. A business can handle sudden spikes in customer activity without building new infrastructure.

Another reason is **cost efficiency**. Cloud computing allows organizations to pay only for what they use. This reduces upfront costs and makes advanced technology accessible to smaller organizations that could not afford their own data centers. Cloud services also shift maintenance responsibilities to providers who specialize in managing infrastructure.

Cloud computing also improves **accessibility and collaboration**. Data stored in the cloud can be accessed from different locations and devices, as long as users have permission. This enables remote learning, telemedicine, global collaboration, and real-time data sharing across teams and industries.

Despite its convenience, cloud computing does not eliminate the need for data centers. In fact, cloud computing depends on large networks of data centers distributed around the world. These data centers work together to balance workloads, store backups, and ensure reliability. When one data center experiences an issue, others can take over, maintaining service continuity.

Some organizations choose a **hybrid approach**, combining cloud services with their own private data centers. This allows them to keep sensitive data on-site while using cloud resources for flexibility and scalability. Hybrid models are common in healthcare, government, and education, where privacy and control are especially important.

Cloud computing also plays a critical role in artificial intelligence. AI systems require massive computing power and storage, which cloud platforms provide through specialized data centers optimized for AI workloads. These systems allow organizations to train and deploy AI models without building their own advanced infrastructure.

Security remains a shared responsibility in cloud environments. Cloud providers secure the underlying data centers and infrastructure, while users are responsible for managing access, permissions, and appropriate data use. Understanding this shared responsibility helps organizations protect data effectively.

Environmental impact is another important consideration. Large cloud providers invest in energy efficiency and renewable power for their data centers. As cloud usage grows, sustainability becomes a key factor in how data centers are designed and operated.

Understanding the relationship between cloud computing and data centers helps readers move beyond the idea of the cloud as something abstract or invisible. Cloud services are grounded in real infrastructure, real energy use, and real systems working together across the globe.

Together, data centers and cloud computing form the backbone of modern digital life. They enable data storage, support artificial intelligence, and make data-driven decisions possible across every industry. Recognizing how they work together empowers readers to better understand the systems shaping the modern world.

Cloud Computing and Data Centers: How They Work Together

Chapter Summary

This chapter explains the difference between data centers and cloud computing, and how they work together to support modern digital systems. Data centers are physical facilities that store and process data using servers, networking equipment, power systems, and cooling infrastructure. Cloud computing is a service model that delivers computing resources—such as storage, processing power, and software—over the internet using those data centers.

The chapter clarifies that data centers are the foundation, while cloud computing is the method by which computing resources are accessed and shared. Cloud computing allows organizations to use technology without owning or maintaining physical servers, offering flexibility, scalability, and cost efficiency. This has transformed how schools, businesses, governments, and startups operate.

Cloud services depend on networks of data centers distributed around the world. These centers work together to balance workloads, provide backups, and ensure reliability. Many organizations use hybrid models that combine cloud services with private data centers, especially when privacy and control are important. Cloud computing also plays a major role in artificial intelligence by providing the large-scale computing power required for AI systems. The chapter emphasizes that cloud services are grounded in real infrastructure, shared security responsibility, and environmental considerations.

Quiz: Chapter 16

Instructions: Answer the questions below.

1. What is a data center?
2. What is cloud computing?

3. How are data centers and cloud computing different?
4. In simple terms, how do data centers and cloud computing work together?
5. Why is scalability an important benefit of cloud computing?
6. True or False: Cloud computing eliminates the need for data centers.
7. How does cloud computing help reduce costs for organizations?
8. What is a hybrid computing model?
9. Why is cloud computing important for artificial intelligence systems?
10. What does "shared responsibility" mean in cloud security?

Worksheet: Cloud Computing & Data Centers

Part A: Core Understanding

1. In your own words, explain the difference between a data center and cloud computing.
2. List three benefits of cloud computing mentioned in the chapter.
3. Why are data centers still necessary even when using the cloud?

Part B: Real-World Applications

4. Give one example of how a school or business might use cloud computing.
5. Why might an organization choose a hybrid approach instead of cloud-only?
6. How does cloud computing support collaboration and remote access?

Part C: Responsibility and Impact

7. Who is responsible for security in a cloud environment?
8. Why is understanding shared responsibility important for protecting data?
9. What environmental concerns are connected to cloud computing and data centers?
10. Write one question you would ask before choosing a cloud service provider.

Answer Key

Quiz Answers

1. A physical facility that stores and processes data using computer systems.
2. A service model that delivers computing resources over the internet.
3. Data centers are physical buildings; cloud computing is how resources are delivered.
4. Data centers provide the hardware, and cloud computing provides access to it.
5. Because systems can expand or shrink based on demand.
6. **False**
7. Organizations pay only for what they use instead of buying hardware.
8. A system that combines cloud services with private data centers.
9. It provides large-scale computing power and storage for AI models.
10. Cloud providers secure infrastructure, while users manage access and data use.

Worksheet Sample Answers

Part A

1. Data centers are buildings with servers; cloud computing lets people use those servers online.
2. Scalability, cost efficiency, accessibility.
3. Because cloud services run on physical machines.

Part B

4. A school using cloud platforms for online learning.
5. To keep sensitive data on-site while using cloud flexibility.
6. By allowing data to be accessed from different locations and devices.

Part C

7. Both the cloud provider and the user.
8. Because mismanaged access can still cause data breaches.
9. Energy use and environmental impact.
10. How does this provider protect data and manage sustainability? (answers may vary)

Chapter 17

AI Data Centers: Powering Artificial Intelligence

As artificial intelligence becomes more advanced and widely used, traditional data centers are no longer sufficient on their own. AI systems require enormous computing power, specialized hardware, and highly optimized environments. This need has led to the rise of **AI data centers**, a new generation of facilities designed specifically to support artificial intelligence workloads.

An AI data center is a specialized type of data center built to handle the intense demands of training and running AI systems. Unlike standard data centers, which focus primarily on storage and general computing tasks, AI data centers are optimized for large-scale data processing, complex calculations, and continuous learning operations.

One of the defining features of AI data centers is their use of **specialized chips**. Traditional computer processors are designed for general tasks, but AI systems rely on chips such as graphics processing units and other accelerators that can perform many calculations at the same time. These chips allow AI models to analyze massive datasets, recognize patterns, and make predictions far more efficiently than standard processors.

AI data centers are essential for **training artificial intelligence models**. Training involves feeding large volumes of data into a model so it can learn relationships, patterns, and behaviors. This process can take days, weeks, or even months, depending on the size of the model and the complexity of the data. AI data centers provide the computing power and storage needed to complete this training at scale.

Once AI models are trained, AI data centers also support **deployment and inference**. Inference is the process of using a trained AI model to generate results, such as answering questions, recognizing images, or making recommendations. These tasks must often happen quickly, sometimes in real time, which requires high-performance systems and efficient data flow.

Energy and cooling play a critical role in AI data centers. AI workloads generate significant heat due to the intensity of processing. Advanced cooling systems are required to maintain stable temperatures and prevent equipment damage. As a result, AI data centers are often designed with innovative cooling technologies and careful energy management strategies.

Reliability is especially important for AI data centers because many AI-powered services are used continuously. Healthcare diagnostics, financial systems, transportation networks, and communication platforms all depend on AI systems running without interruption. To ensure reliability, AI data centers use redundant power supplies, backup systems, and continuous monitoring.

AI data centers also support **collaboration and connectivity**. They are connected through high-speed networks that allow data to move efficiently between systems and regions. This connectivity enables global AI services, distributed training, and shared research efforts across organizations and industries.

Security and data protection remain central concerns in AI data centers. Because AI systems often rely on sensitive data, strong safeguards are required to protect information from misuse or breaches. Access controls, encryption, and monitoring systems help ensure that data remains secure while supporting large-scale AI operations.

The growth of AI data centers has raised important questions about sustainability. AI systems consume significant energy, and data center operators are increasingly focused on reducing environmental impact. Efforts include using renewable energy, improving efficiency, and designing facilities that minimize resource consumption.

AI data centers are not only technological facilities; they are strategic assets. Nations, companies, and institutions invest heavily in AI data center infrastructure because it determines their ability to compete, innovate, and lead in an AI-driven world. Access to advanced AI infrastructure shapes what systems can be built and how quickly progress can occur.

Understanding AI data centers helps readers see that artificial intelligence is not just software or algorithms. It is supported by real-world infrastructure, physical resources, and human expertise. AI data centers are the engines that transform raw data into intelligent systems capable of influencing decisions across every industry.

As artificial intelligence continues to evolve, AI data centers will remain central to its growth. They represent the intersection of data, hardware, energy, and intelligence—making them one of the most important components of the modern digital ecosystem.

AI Data Centers: Powering Artificial Intelligence

Chapter Summary

This chapter explains the role of AI data centers and why they are essential to modern artificial intelligence systems. As AI becomes more advanced, it requires far more computing power than traditional systems. AI data centers are specialized facilities designed to handle the intense processing, storage, and energy demands of training and running AI models.

AI data centers differ from traditional data centers by using specialized hardware, such as advanced processing chips that can perform many calculations simultaneously. These facilities support both AI training—where models learn from massive datasets—and inference, where trained models generate real-time results such as predictions, recommendations, or responses.

The chapter highlights the importance of energy management, cooling, reliability, security, and connectivity in AI data centers. Because AI-powered services often operate continuously, these facilities are designed with redundancy and monitoring to ensure uninterrupted operation. Sustainability is also a growing concern, with efforts focused on renewable energy and efficiency. The chapter concludes by emphasizing that AI data centers are not just technical facilities, but strategic assets that support innovation, competitiveness, and progress in an AI-driven world.

Quiz: Chapter 17

Instructions: Answer the questions below.

1. What is an AI data center?
2. How do AI data centers differ from traditional data centers?
3. Why do AI systems require specialized chips?
4. What is AI training, and why is it resource-intensive?
5. What is inference in artificial intelligence?
6. True or False: AI data centers are only used during model training.
7. Why are cooling systems especially important in AI data centers?
8. How do AI data centers ensure reliability?
9. Why is sustainability a concern for AI data centers?
10. Why are AI data centers considered strategic assets?

Worksheet: Understanding AI Data Centers

Part A: Core Concepts

1. In your own words, explain why AI needs specialized data centers.

2. List three key components or features of AI data centers.
3. Why is physical infrastructure still important for artificial intelligence?

Part B: AI Operations and Performance

4. Describe the difference between AI training and inference.
5. Why must inference often happen quickly or in real time?
6. How does high-speed connectivity support AI data centers?

Part C: Responsibility, Sustainability, and the Future

7. Why is security critical in AI data centers?
8. What environmental challenges do AI data centers create?
9. How can organizations reduce the environmental impact of AI infrastructure?
10. Write one reason why understanding AI data centers helps people better understand AI systems.

Answer Key

Quiz Answers

1. A specialized data center designed to support artificial intelligence workloads.
2. They are optimized for large-scale processing, AI training, and inference.
3. Because AI requires many calculations to be performed simultaneously.
4. Training involves teaching AI models using large datasets and complex computations.
5. Using a trained AI model to produce outputs such as predictions or answers.
6. **False**
7. Because AI workloads generate large amounts of heat.
8. Through redundancy, backup systems, and continuous monitoring.
9. Because AI systems consume significant energy.
10. They determine an organization's ability to innovate and compete in AI.

Worksheet Sample Answers

Part A

1. Because AI needs more power and specialized hardware than regular systems.
2. Specialized chips, advanced cooling, high-speed networks.
3. Because AI runs on real machines using real energy and hardware.

Part B

4. Training teaches models; inference uses trained models to produce results.
5. Because many AI services must respond immediately to users.
6. It allows data to move efficiently between systems and regions.

Part C
7. Because AI systems often handle sensitive or valuable data.
8. High energy use and environmental impact.
9. By using renewable energy and improving efficiency.
10. It shows that AI depends on real infrastructure, not just software. (answers may vary)

Teacher Preface

How to Use This Book in the Classroom

Data Drives Decisions in Every Industry was written to help students understand one of the most important forces shaping the modern world: **data**. Today's students grow up surrounded by digital systems, yet many do not fully understand how data influences decisions in education, healthcare, business, government, and everyday life. This book was created to close that gap through clear explanations, real-world context, and responsible discussion.

This text is designed as a **foundational data literacy resource**, not a technical manual. It does not require prior knowledge of computer science, programming, or advanced mathematics. Instead, it focuses on helping students understand how data is collected, stored, protected, interpreted, and applied across industries. The goal is to build understanding, critical thinking, and informed awareness.

Intended Audience

This book is suitable for:

- Middle school and high school students
- Community college and introductory college courses
- Career and technical education programs
- Educators introducing AI, data literacy, or digital systems
- General readers seeking clarity about data-driven systems

The content is written in an accessible, textbook-style format that supports both guided instruction and independent reading.

Educational Goals

This book helps students:

- Understand what data is and where it comes from
- Recognize how data supports decision-making
- See how data is used differently across industries
- Learn the importance of data quality, protection, and ethics

- Understand the physical infrastructure behind digital systems, including data centers and AI data centers
- Develop critical awareness of data's role in everyday life

By the end of the book, students should be able to explain **how data moves from raw information to real-world decisions** and why responsible data use matters.

How the Book Is Structured

The book is organized in four learning phases:

The opening chapters introduce the fundamentals of data, including its sources, storage, protection, and quality. These chapters establish a shared vocabulary and conceptual foundation.

The middle chapters explore how data drives decisions across major industries such as education, healthcare, business, government, and daily life. These sections help students connect abstract concepts to familiar systems.

Later chapters address ethical responsibility and the future of data-driven decision-making, encouraging thoughtful discussion about trust, fairness, and accountability.

The final chapters focus on infrastructure, explaining data centers, cloud computing, and AI data centers. These chapters reveal the physical systems that make digital and AI-driven decisions possible.

Classroom Use Suggestions

Teachers may use this book:

- As a full-course text for data literacy or AI awareness
- As a supplemental text alongside technology, business, or social studies courses
- For discussion-based learning focused on ethics, responsibility, and systems thinking
- For cross-disciplinary instruction linking technology with real-world applications

Chapters are written to stand alone, allowing instructors to select sections that best fit their curriculum.

Discussion and Reflection

The book encourages reflection rather than memorization. Students are invited to think about how data affects their own lives and communities. Teachers may pair chapters with:

- Class discussions
- Short reflection writing
- Group projects exploring data use in local systems
- Case studies based on real-world scenarios

Responsible Perspective

This book presents data and artificial intelligence without fear or hype. It emphasizes that data-driven systems are tools created by humans and guided by human values. Ethical responsibility, transparency, and informed participation are central themes throughout the text.

Closing Note to Educators

Data literacy is becoming as essential as reading, writing, and numeracy. By helping students understand how data drives decisions, educators empower them to navigate the modern world with confidence, awareness, and responsibility.

This book is intended to support that mission.

Glossary

Letter A

1. Access Time

The amount of time it takes for an AI system or computer to locate and retrieve data from memory or storage. Access time affects how quickly megabytes of data can be used during AI processing.

2. Activation Data

Intermediate data generated inside an AI model while it is running. Activation data is stored temporarily in memory and often measured in megabytes during model execution.

3. Adaptive Storage

A storage approach that automatically adjusts how data is stored or moved based on usage patterns. In AI systems, adaptive storage helps manage large volumes of megabytes efficiently.

4.Algorithm

A set of instructions or rules that tells a computer or system how to solve a problem or complete a task.

5. Algorithmic Data Size

The total amount of data an algorithm needs to operate effectively. In AI, this size is often measured in megabytes or larger units, depending on model complexity.

6. Allocation (Memory Allocation)

The process of assigning a specific number of megabytes in memory or storage for an AI task, model, or dataset.

7. Analytics Dataset

A structured collection of data used for analysis or AI training. The size of an analytics dataset is commonly measured in megabytes, gigabytes, or more.

8.ANI (Artificial Narrow Intelligence)

Artificial Narrow Intelligence refers to AI systems designed to perform **one specific task or a narrow set of tasks** rather than general intelligence. ANI systems rely on data stored and processed in memory and storage measured in **megabytes, gigabytes, or more**. Examples include image recognition, speech-to-text, recommendation systems, and chatbots. ANI does not understand beyond its training scope, but it can process large amounts of data efficiently within its defined function.

9. Annotation Storage

The space required to store labels, tags, or explanations added to AI training data. These annotations contribute additional megabytes to total dataset size.

Artificial Intelligence (AI)
Computer systems designed to perform tasks that normally require human intelligence, such as learning, recognizing patterns, and making decisions.

10. Artificial Neural Network (ANN) Size

The total memory footprint of a neural network, including weights, biases, and parameters. ANN size is often described in megabytes when discussing model efficiency.

11. Asset Compression

The process of reducing the number of megabytes required to store AI-related files such as models, images, or datasets without losing essential information.

12. Available Memory

The amount of free memory, measured in megabytes, that an AI system can still use to load data, run models, or perform computations.

Letter B

1. Bandwidth

The amount of data that can be transferred between systems in a given time. In AI systems, bandwidth determines how quickly megabytes of data can move between storage, memory, and processors.

2. Batch Processing

A method where AI systems process large groups of data all at once instead of one item at a time. Batch processing often involves handling many megabytes of data in a single operation.

3.Bias (in Data)

When data unfairly represents certain groups or outcomes, often because of how it was collected or selected.

4. Binary Encoding

The process of representing information using binary values (0s and 1s). All megabytes of AI data are ultimately stored and transmitted using binary encoding.

5. Bit Depth

The number of bits used to represent a single piece of data, such as a pixel or audio sample. Higher bit depth increases data quality but also increases the number of megabytes required.

6. Bitmap Data

A type of image data where each pixel is stored as a set of bits. Bitmap images can quickly grow in size, consuming large numbers of megabytes in AI vision systems.

7. Buffer Memory

Temporary memory used to hold data while it is being transferred or processed. Buffers store data in chunks measured in megabytes to keep AI systems running smoothly.

8. Bulk Data Storage

Large-scale storage designed to hold massive datasets used for AI training or analysis. Bulk storage capacity is measured in megabytes, gigabytes, or larger units.

9. Byte Stream

A continuous flow of bytes transmitted or processed by a system. AI applications often analyze byte streams that accumulate into megabytes of data.

10. Bytecode

An intermediate form of program code that is easier for machines to execute than human-written code. Bytecode files occupy storage space measured in megabytes.

11. Byzantine Fault Tolerance (BFT)

A system property that allows AI or distributed systems to continue functioning even when some components fail or act unpredictably. Implementing BFT requires additional data handling and storage overhead measured in megabytes.

Letter C

1. Cache Memory

A small, high-speed memory area that stores frequently used data so the processor can access it faster. Cache helps reduce the time needed to move megabytes of data from main memory or storage.

2. Capacity Planning

The process of estimating how much memory and storage an AI system will need. Capacity planning ensures there are enough megabytes available to handle data, models, and future growth.

3. Checkpoint File

A saved snapshot of an AI model during training. Checkpoint files are stored in memory or storage and often consume many megabytes so training can resume without starting over.

4. Chunking

The practice of breaking large datasets into smaller pieces. Chunking helps AI systems process megabytes of data more efficiently by handling them in manageable parts.

5.Cloud Computing
A way of accessing data, software, and computing power over the internet instead of using a local computer or server.

6. Cloud Storage

A method of storing data on remote servers accessed through the internet. Cloud storage manages files measured in megabytes and allows AI systems to scale beyond local hardware limits.

7. Compression

The process of reducing the size of data so it uses fewer megabytes. Compression helps AI systems store, transfer, and process data more efficiently.

8. Compute Load

The amount of processing work required to run an AI task. Compute load often increases as the number of megabytes being processed grows.

9. Context Window

The amount of data an AI model can consider at one time. Context windows consume memory measured in megabytes, especially in language and vision models.

10. Corpus

A large collection of text or data used to train AI models. A corpus is usually measured in megabytes or larger units depending on its size.

11. CUDA Memory

Specialized memory used by GPUs to accelerate AI computations. CUDA memory holds model data and intermediate results measured in megabytes during processing.

Letter D

1. Data Allocation

The process of assigning a specific amount of memory or storage for data use. In AI systems, data allocation determines how many megabytes are reserved for datasets, models, or tasks.

2. Data Buffer

A temporary storage area that holds data while it is being transferred or processed. Data buffers manage megabytes of information to keep AI systems running smoothly.

3. Data Compression

A technique used to reduce the size of data so it consumes fewer megabytes. AI systems use data compression to save storage space and speed up data transfer.

4. Data Footprint

The total amount of data an AI system uses, including datasets, models, and temporary files. A data footprint is measured in megabytes, gigabytes, or more.

5. Data Loader

A software component that loads data into memory for AI training or inference. Data loaders handle batches of data measured in megabytes.

Data Center
A physical facility that houses computers, servers, and storage systems used to store and process data.

Data Quality
A measure of how accurate, complete, consistent, and up-to-date data is.

Data Protection
Methods used to keep data safe from unauthorized access, misuse, or loss.

Data-Driven Decision-Making
The practice of using data and evidence to guide choices instead of relying only on intuition or opinion.

Database
An organized digital system that stores large amounts of data in a structured way.

6. Data Migration

The process of moving data from one storage system to another. During AI system upgrades, data migration may involve transferring large numbers of megabytes.

7. Data Throughput

The rate at which data is processed or transferred by a system. Higher throughput allows AI systems to move more megabytes efficiently.

8. Dataset Size

The total amount of data in a dataset used for AI training or testing. Dataset size is commonly measured in megabytes or larger units.

9. Deep Learning Model Size

The amount of memory required to store a deep learning model, including its parameters and weights. Model size is often described in megabytes to assess efficiency.

10. Disk Storage

Long-term storage used to save files, datasets, and AI models. Disk storage capacity and usage are measured in megabytes, gigabytes, or terabytes.

Letter E

1. Edge Computing

A computing approach where data is processed closer to where it is generated rather than sent to a central server. Edge computing reduces how many megabytes must be transferred over networks.

2. Embedding Size

The amount of memory required to store vector representations used by AI models. Embedding size is often measured in megabytes and affects model performance and storage needs.

3. Encoded Data

Data that has been converted into a specific format for storage or transmission. Encoded data occupies megabytes depending on the encoding method used.

4. Encoding Scheme

A rule set that defines how data is represented digitally, such as text or images. Different encoding schemes can increase or reduce the number of megabytes required.

5. Encrypted Storage

Storage that protects data by converting it into a secure format. Encryption may slightly increase the number of megabytes used due to added security information

6.End-to-End Data Pipeline

The full path data takes from collection to processing and storage. Each stage of the pipeline manages data volumes measured in megabytes.

8. Energy Efficiency (AI Systems)

A measure of how much energy an AI system uses to process data. Systems that move and store fewer megabytes are often more energy efficient.

Ethical Data Use
Handling data in a fair, responsible, and transparent way that respects privacy and human rights.

9. Execution Memory

The memory required while a program or AI model is running. Execution memory usage is tracked in megabytes during runtime.

10. External Storage

Storage devices located outside a computer, such as USB drives or external hard drives. External storage capacity is measured in megabytes and larger units.

11. Extracted Features

Important data patterns identified by AI models during processing. Extracted features are stored temporarily or permanently in memory measured in megabytes.

Letter F

1. Feature Map

A structured output produced by AI models, especially in image and signal processing. Feature maps are stored in memory and can consume significant megabytes during computation.

2. Feature Scaling

The process of adjusting data values to a consistent range before training an AI model. Feature scaling affects how efficiently megabytes of data are processed and stored.

3. File Allocation Table (FAT)

A file system structure that tracks where files are stored on a disk. FAT helps manage how megabytes are organized and retrieved from storage.

4. File Compression Format

A standardized way to reduce file size so it uses fewer megabytes. Compression formats help AI systems store and transfer data efficiently.

5. File System Cache

A temporary memory area that stores frequently accessed files. File system caches reduce repeated access to storage and manage megabytes more efficiently.

6. Floating-Point Data

Numerical data that includes decimal values and is commonly used in AI calculations. Floating-point data requires more bits per value, increasing memory usage measured in megabytes.

7. Frame Buffer

A region of memory that stores image or video frames before they are displayed or processed. Frame buffers often consume large numbers of megabytes in AI vision systems.

8. Fragmentation

A condition where data is stored in scattered locations instead of one continuous block. Fragmentation can reduce storage efficiency even when megabytes appear available.

9. Free Memory

The amount of unused memory available for programs or AI tasks. Free memory is measured in megabytes and determines how much additional data can be loaded.

10. Full Dataset Load

The act of loading an entire dataset into memory at once. This approach can require large amounts of megabytes and is common in AI training scenarios.

Letter G

1. Garbage Collection

An automatic memory-management process that frees memory no longer in use. Garbage collection helps reclaim megabytes so AI programs can continue running efficiently.

2. Generalization Data

Data used to test how well an AI model performs on new, unseen inputs. Storing and evaluating generalization data requires additional megabytes beyond training data.

3. Gigabyte (GB)

A larger unit of data measurement equal to 1,024 megabytes (or commonly approximated as 1,000 MB). Gigabytes are used when datasets or models grow beyond megabyte scale.

4. Graph Data Structure

A way of organizing data using nodes and connections. Graph-based AI systems store graph data in memory and storage measured in megabytes.

5. GPU Memory

Specialized memory used by graphics processing units to accelerate AI workloads. GPU memory holds model parameters and data batches measured in megabytes.

6. Gradient Data

Numerical values calculated during AI training to update model parameters. Gradient data is stored temporarily in memory and contributes to overall megabyte usage.

7. Granularity

The level of detail at which data is stored or processed. Finer granularity often increases the number of megabytes required.

8. Greedy Algorithm

An algorithm that makes the best immediate choice at each step. Greedy algorithms may reduce memory usage by limiting how many megabytes of data must be stored at once.

9. Ground Truth Data

Correct, labeled data used to train or evaluate AI systems. Ground truth datasets are stored in files measured in megabytes or larger units.

10. Growth Rate (Data)

The speed at which data size increases over time. In AI systems, a high data growth rate means storage needs measured in megabytes can expand quickly.

Letter H

1. Hard Disk Capacity

The total amount of data a hard disk can store. Capacity is measured in megabytes and larger units.

2. Hardware Acceleration

The use of specialized hardware to speed up AI processing. Acceleration often reduces how long megabytes of data stay in memory.

3. Hash Table

A data structure that stores information for fast lookup. Hash tables occupy memory measured in megabytes in large AI systems.

4. Hierarchical Storage

A storage design that uses multiple layers such as RAM, disk, and cloud. Each layer manages data measured in megabytes.

5. High-Dimensional Data

Data with many features or variables. High-dimensional datasets often require large numbers of megabytes.

6. Host Memory

Main system memory used by the CPU. Host memory stores AI data and models measured in megabytes.

7. Hybrid Storage

A combination of different storage types working together. Hybrid storage systems manage megabytes across multiple devices.

8. Hyperparameter Storage

Memory used to store configuration values for AI models. These settings are saved in files measured in megabytes.

9. Hyperscale Data

Extremely large datasets used by major AI systems. Hyperscale data is tracked from megabytes up to much larger units.

10. Heuristic Data

Information used by AI systems to guide decision-making. Heuristic data contributes to the overall data size in megabytes.

Letter I

1. Image Dataset Size

The total amount of storage required for image data. Size is measured in megabytes or more.

2.Inference (AI)
The process of using a trained AI model to produce answers, predictions, or results.

3. Inference Memory

The memory used when an AI model is making predictions. Inference memory usage is tracked in megabytes.

4.Infrastructure (Digital)
The physical and technical systems—such as data centers, networks, and servers—that support digital services.

5. Input Buffer

A temporary area where incoming data is stored. Input buffers hold megabytes before processing begins.

6.. Intermediate Data

Data produced during processing steps. Intermediate data can significantly increase memory usage in megabytes.

7. Index File

A file that helps locate data quickly. Index files use additional megabytes to improve performance.

8. Information Density

The amount of useful data stored within a given size. Higher density means more information per megabyte.

9. Initialization Data

Data loaded when an AI system starts. Initialization data occupies memory measured in megabytes.

10. In-Memory Processing

Processing data directly in RAM instead of storage. This approach uses large amounts of memory measured in megabytes.

11. Input Feature Size

The amount of data required to represent input features. Feature size affects how many megabytes are needed.

12. Instruction Cache

A small memory area that stores frequently used instructions. Instruction caches manage small but critical megabytes.

Letter J

1. Job Queue

A list of tasks waiting to be processed. Job queues may store task data measured in megabytes.

2. Joint Dataset

A dataset created by combining multiple sources. Joint datasets often increase total size in megabytes.

3. JSON Data Size

The amount of storage required for data stored in JSON format. JSON files can grow quickly in megabytes.

4. Jitter Buffer

A temporary storage area that smooths data flow. Jitter buffers store megabytes during real-time processing.

5. Job Scheduler

A system that decides when tasks run. Schedulers manage memory and data measured in megabytes.

6. Just-in-Time Processing

Processing data only when needed. This approach can reduce how many megabytes are stored at once.

7. Joint Memory Allocation

Memory shared across multiple AI tasks. Joint allocation must carefully manage available megabytes.

8. Java Bytecode Size

The storage size of compiled Java programs. Bytecode files occupy megabytes on disk.

9. Job Metadata

Information describing AI tasks. Metadata adds additional megabytes to total system storage.

10. Junction Storage Point

A logical link between storage locations. Junctions help organize data measured in megabytes.

Letter K

1. Kernel Memory

Memory reserved for core system operations. Kernel memory usage is tracked in megabytes.

2. Key-Value Store

A data storage method that pairs keys with values. Large key-value stores consume many megabytes.

3. Knowledge Base Size

The total amount of stored knowledge in an AI system. Size is measured in megabytes or larger units.

4. K-Means Dataset Size

The amount of data used in clustering algorithms. Dataset size affects memory usage in megabytes.

5. Keras Model Size

The storage required for AI models built with Keras. Model size is measured in megabytes.

6. Keyframe Data

Important frames selected from video data. Keyframe storage contributes to total megabyte usage.

7. Kernel Cache

A cache used by the operating system kernel. Kernel caches store frequently used data in megabytes.

8. Knowledge Graph Storage

Memory used to store relationships between data points. Knowledge graphs require significant megabytes.

9. Kinetic Data Stream

Continuously changing data from sensors or systems. These streams generate growing megabytes over time.

10. K-Nearest Neighbor Memory Usage

The memory required by nearest-neighbor algorithms. Memory use increases as datasets grow in megabytes.

Letter L

1. **Latency**
   The delay between requesting data and receiving it. Latency affects how quickly megabytes move through AI systems.
2. **Layer Output Size**
   The amount of data produced by a neural network layer. Output size is measured in megabytes during processing.
3. **Load Balancing**
   Distributing work across systems so no single device is overloaded. Balancing helps manage megabytes efficiently.
4. **Local Storage**
   Data stored on a device rather than the cloud. Local storage capacity is measured in megabytes.
5. **Log File Size**
   The amount of storage used by system logs. Logs can accumulate many megabytes over time.
6. **Loss History Data**
   Stored values showing how model error changes during training. Loss history consumes megabytes.
7. **Low-Precision Data**
   Data stored using fewer bits per value. Low-precision formats reduce megabyte usage.
8. **Labeled Dataset**
   Data that includes tags or labels for AI training. Labels increase total dataset size in megabytes.

9. **Linear Model Size**
   The storage required for a linear AI model. Size is measured in megabytes.
10. **Load Time**
   The time required to bring data or models into memory. Load time depends on megabytes involved.

Letter M

1. **Machine Learning**
   A type of AI that allows systems to learn patterns from data and improve over time.

2. **Memory Allocation**
   Assigning a specific amount of memory for tasks. Allocation is tracked in megabytes.
3. **Memory Footprint**
   The total memory an AI program uses. Footprint is measured in megabytes.
4. **Metadata Size**
   The storage used by descriptive information about data. Metadata adds extra megabytes.
5. **Mini-Batch Size**
   The amount of data processed at once during training. Batch size affects megabyte usage.
6. **Model Checkpoint Size**
   The storage required for saved training states. Checkpoints often consume many megabytes.
7. **Model Compression**
   Reducing model size while preserving performance. Compression lowers megabytes required.
8. **Model Parameters**
   Values learned by an AI model. Parameter storage contributes to total megabytes.
9. **Memory Bandwidth**
   The rate at which memory transfers data. Bandwidth affects how fast megabytes move.
10. **Multimodal Dataset**
   Data combining text, images, audio, or video. Multimodal data uses large megabytes.
11. **Mutable Data**
   Data that changes during processing. Mutable data can increase temporary megabyte usage.

Letter N

1. **Network Bandwidth**
   The capacity of a network connection. Bandwidth controls how many megabytes can be transferred.

2. **Neural Network Size**
   The total storage required for a neural network. Size is measured in megabytes.
3. **Node Memory**
   Memory available on a computing node. Node memory limits megabytes per task.
4. **Normalization Data**
   Values used to scale data consistently. Normalization adds to dataset megabytes.
5. **Non-Volatile Memory**
   Memory that retains data without power. Capacity is measured in megabytes.
6. **Numerical Precision**
   The detail level of stored numbers. Higher precision increases megabytes.
7. **Noise Data**
   Unwanted or random information in datasets. Noise increases data size in megabytes.
8. **Neural Activation Size**
   Memory used to store neuron outputs. Activation size is measured in megabytes.
9. **Network Transfer Size**
   The amount of data sent across a network. Transfer size is tracked in megabytes.
10. **Node Cache**
    Temporary storage on a node for faster access. Cache size uses megabytes.

Letter O

1. **Object Storage**
   A storage method that manages data as objects. Capacity is measured in megabytes.
2. **Offline Dataset**
   Data stored locally rather than streamed. Offline datasets occupy megabytes.
3. **On-Device Storage**
   Storage located on the AI device itself. On-device capacity is measured in megabytes.
4. **Operational Memory**
   Memory used during active AI operations. Usage is tracked in megabytes.
5. **Optimization Data**
   Information used to improve model performance. Optimization data uses megabytes.
6. **Output Buffer**
   Temporary storage for results before delivery. Buffers hold megabytes.
7. **Overhead Data**
   Extra data required for system operation. Overhead increases total megabytes.
8. **Object Detection Output Size**
   The amount of data produced by detection models. Output size is measured in megabytes.
9. **Online Storage**
   Storage accessible via the internet. Online storage limits are measured in megabytes.
10. **Open Dataset Size**
    The storage footprint of publicly available datasets. Size is measured in megabytes.

Letter P

1. **Parameter Count**
   The total number of model values. Count correlates with megabytes required.
2. **Persistent Storage**
   Long-term storage that retains data. Capacity is measured in megabytes.
3. **Pipeline Buffer**
   Temporary storage between processing stages. Buffers manage megabytes in motion.
4. **Preprocessing Data**
   Data created while preparing datasets. Preprocessing adds megabytes.
5. **Precision Reduction**
   Lowering numeric detail to save space. Reduction decreases megabyte usage.
6. **Prediction Output Size**
   The amount of data produced by model predictions. Size is measured in megabytes.
7. **Primary Memory**
   Main system memory used for processing. Capacity is measured in megabytes.
8. **Processing Overhead**
   Extra resources needed during computation. Overhead increases megabyte usage.
9. **Profiling Data**
   Information collected to analyze performance. Profiling data uses megabytes.
10. **Paged Memory**
    Memory divided into fixed-size blocks. Paging manages megabytes efficiently.

Letter Q

1. **Quantization**
   A technique that reduces numerical precision to lower memory usage. Quantization helps AI models use fewer megabytes.
2. **Query Cache**
   Stored results from previous searches or requests. Query caches save megabytes by avoiding repeated computation.
3. **Query Latency**
   The time it takes to retrieve data after a request. Latency depends on how many megabytes must be accessed.
4. **Queue Buffer**
   A temporary holding area for data waiting to be processed. Buffers store megabytes in order.
5. **Quick Access Memory**
   Memory designed for fast retrieval. It handles megabytes needed immediately by AI tasks.
6. **Quantitative Dataset**
   Data made up of numerical values. These datasets are stored and measured in megabytes.
7. **Query Result Size**
   The amount of data returned from a query. Result size is measured in megabytes.

8. **Quorum Storage**
   A distributed storage method requiring agreement across systems. Data is replicated in megabytes.
9. **Quality Metrics Data**
   Information used to measure model performance. Metrics consume storage in megabytes.
10. **Quantized Model Size**
    The reduced size of an AI model after quantization. Size is typically measured in megabytes.

Letter R

1. **RAM Usage**
   The amount of active memory in use. RAM usage is tracked in megabytes.
2. **Read Throughput**
   The speed at which data is read from storage. Throughput affects how fast megabytes are accessed.
3. **Real-Time Processing**
   Processing data immediately as it arrives. Real-time systems manage megabytes continuously.
4. **Recursive Memory Use**
   Memory consumption during repeated function calls. Usage accumulates in megabytes.
5. **Redundant Storage**
   Extra copies of data kept for reliability. Redundancy increases total megabytes stored.
6. **Resource Allocation**
   Assigning system resources like memory and storage. Allocation is measured in megabytes.
7. **Runtime Memory**
   Memory required while a program is running. Runtime memory usage is tracked in megabytes.
8. **Raw Dataset Size**
   The size of unprocessed data. Raw datasets often require many megabytes.
9. **Read-Only Memory Footprint**
   The storage space used by non-modifiable data. Footprint is measured in megabytes.
10. **Retrieval Speed**
    How quickly stored data can be accessed. Speed depends on the number of megabytes involved.

Letter S

1. **Sample Size**
   The number of data examples used in AI training. Larger samples increase megabytes.

2. **Scalable Storage**
   Storage that grows with demand. Scalability supports increasing megabytes.
3. **Sensor**
   A device that collects data by detecting changes such as motion, temperature, sound, or light.
4. **Server**
   A powerful computer that stores data and provides services to other computers or devices.
5. **Serialized Data Size**
   The storage size of data converted into a transferable format. Size is measured in megabytes.
6. **Shared Memory**
   Memory accessible by multiple processes. Shared memory usage is tracked in megabytes.
7. **Snapshot Size**
   The storage required for saved system states. Snapshots consume megabytes.

8.Sparse Data Representation
A storage method that saves space when data contains many empty values. Sparsity reduces megabytes.

9.Storage Capacity
The total amount of data a system can store. Capacity is measured in megabytes or more.

10.Streaming Data Buffer
Temporary storage for incoming data streams. Buffers handle megabytes in motion.

11.System Cache
Memory that stores frequently used data. Caches manage megabytes for faster access.

12.Synchronization Data
Information used to keep systems aligned. Sync data adds to total megabytes.

13.Sensor
A device that collects data by detecting changes such as motion, temperature, sound, or light.
14.Server
A powerful computer that stores data and provides services to other computers or devices.
15.Subscription Data
Data that is accessed continuously through a paid service rather than owned outright.

Letter T

1. **Temporary Storage**
   Short-term storage used during processing. Temporary storage holds megabytes briefly.
2. **Tensor Size**
   The memory required to store multidimensional data structures. Tensor size is measured in megabytes.
3. **Throughput Rate**
   The amount of data processed per unit time. Rate is often described in megabytes per second.
4. **Training Dataset Size**
   The total amount of data used to train AI models. Size is measured in megabytes.
5. **Transfer Buffer**
   Temporary memory used during data movement. Buffers hold megabytes during transfer.
6. **Transactional Storage**
   Storage that ensures data consistency. Transactions add overhead measured in megabytes.
7. **Thread Memory Usage**
   Memory consumed by execution threads. Usage is tracked in megabytes.
8. **Token Storage Size**
   The memory required to store processed tokens. Token data uses megabytes.
9. **Time-Series Data Size**
   The storage footprint of data collected over time. Size increases in megabytes.
10. **Training Checkpoint Size**
    The storage required for saved training states. Checkpoints are measured in megabytes.
11. **Training Data**
    Data used to teach an AI system how to recognize patterns and make predictions.
12. **Transparency**
    The ability to understand how data is collected and how decisions are made using that data.

Letter U

1. **Unified Memory**
   A memory system shared between CPU and GPU. Unified memory manages data in megabytes efficiently across processors.
2. **Upload Size**
   The amount of data sent to storage or the cloud. Upload size is measured in megabytes.
3. **User Data Storage**
   Storage allocated for user-generated files. Capacity is tracked in megabytes.
4. **Utilization Rate**
   The percentage of memory or storage currently in use. Utilization reflects how many megabytes are occupied.

5. **Uncompressed Data Size**
   The size of data before compression. Uncompressed data often uses more megabytes.
6. **Update Payload**
   Data sent during software or model updates. Payload size is measured in megabytes.
7. **Uptime Storage Logs**
   Logs recorded while systems run continuously. Logs accumulate megabytes over time.
8. **Unified Dataset**
   A dataset combined from multiple sources. Size is measured in megabytes.
9. **User Session Memory**
   Memory allocated for active users. Session memory uses megabytes dynamically.
10. **Usage Quota**
    A storage limit set for users or systems. Quotas are defined in megabytes or larger units.

Letter V

1. **Validation Dataset Size**
   The amount of data used to evaluate AI models. Size is measured in megabytes.
2. **Vector Embedding Size**
   The memory required to store numerical representations of data. Size is measured in megabytes.
3. **Virtual Memory**
   A system that extends RAM using disk storage. Virtual memory is managed in megabytes.
4. **Volatile Memory**
   Memory that loses data when power is off. Capacity is measured in megabytes.
5. **Video Dataset Size**
   The storage required for video data. Video datasets consume many megabytes.
6. **Versioned Storage**
   Storage that keeps multiple file versions. Versioning increases megabyte usage.
7. **Vision Model Size**
   The memory footprint of computer vision models. Size is measured in megabytes.
8. **Vector Database Storage**
   Storage used for similarity search data. Vector databases consume large megabytes.
9. **Virtualized Storage**
   Storage abstracted from physical hardware. Capacity is tracked in megabytes.
10. **Volume Capacity**
    The total size of a storage volume. Capacity is measured in megabytes or more.

Letter W

1. **Weight Parameters**
   Learned values in AI models. Weight storage contributes to megabytes used.

2. **Working Memory**
   Memory actively used during processing. Working memory usage is measured in megabytes.
3. **Write Throughput**
   The speed at which data is written to storage. Throughput affects megabytes per second.
4. **Warm Cache**
   Cached data that is already loaded. Warm caches reduce repeated megabyte transfers.
5. **Workflow Data Size**
   The total data used across an AI workflow. Size is measured in megabytes.
6. **Web Dataset Size**
   The storage required for web-based data. Size is tracked in megabytes.
7. **Weight Compression**
   Reducing model weight size to save memory. Compression lowers megabytes used.
8. **Window Size (AI Context)**
   The amount of data processed at once. Window size affects memory megabytes.
9. **Writable Storage**
   Storage that allows data modification. Capacity is measured in megabytes.
10. **Workload Memory Demand**
    The memory required for tasks. Demand is expressed in megabytes.

Letter X

1. **X-Axis Data Size**
   Data stored along one dimension of a dataset. Size contributes to megabytes used.
2. **XML Data Size**
   The storage footprint of XML-formatted data. XML files often use many megabytes.
3. **XOR Encoding**
   A binary operation used in data processing. Encoded data occupies megabytes.
4. **Execution Context Size**
   Memory required during task execution. Size is measured in megabytes.
5. **External Dataset Size**
   The size of data sourced externally. External datasets add megabytes.
6. **Expanded Memory Use**
   Memory growth during processing. Expansion increases megabytes consumed.
7. **Experimental Dataset**
   Data used for testing AI models. Size is measured in megabytes.
8. **Extraction Buffer**
   Temporary storage during data extraction. Buffers store megabytes briefly.
9. **Extended Storage Capacity**
   Additional storage added to a system. Capacity is measured in megabytes.
10. **Explainability Data Size**
    Data used to explain AI decisions. Explainability outputs consume megabytes.

Letter Y

1. **Yield Data Size**
   The amount of useful output data produced. Yield is measured in megabytes.
2. **Yearly Data Growth**
   Annual increase in stored data. Growth is tracked in megabytes.
3. **YAML File Size**
   The storage footprint of YAML configuration files. Size is measured in megabytes.
4. **Y-Axis Feature Size**
   Feature data along a dataset dimension. Size contributes to megabytes.
5. **Young Generation Memory**
   Memory area for newly created data. Usage is measured in megabytes.
6. **Yield Optimization Data**
   Data used to improve output efficiency. Stored in megabytes.
7. **YourAIStudyBuddy Dataset Size**
   The total data used by AI study tools. Size is measured in megabytes.
8. **Yottabyte Reference Scale**
   A conceptual upper scale of data measurement. Used for comparison beyond megabytes.
9. **Yield Metrics Storage**
   Storage used for performance metrics. Metrics consume megabytes.
10. **Yoked Memory Allocation**
    Linked memory regions used together. Allocation is measured in megabytes.

Letter Z

1. **Zero-Copy Memory**
   A method that avoids duplicating data. Zero-copy reduces megabytes in motion.
2. **Zipped Dataset Size**
   The storage size after compression. Zipped files use fewer megabytes.
3. **Zettabyte Scale (Reference)**
   A large-scale data concept. Used to compare growth beyond megabytes.
4. **Zone-Based Storage**
   Storage divided into regions. Zones manage megabytes efficiently.
5. **Z-Score Normalization Data**
   Statistical values used in preprocessing. Data adds megabytes.
6. **Zero Padding**
   Adding placeholder data to inputs. Padding increases memory megabytes.
7. **Zoomed Feature Maps**
   Scaled representations in vision models. Stored in megabytes.
8. **Zonal Cache**
   Cache divided by region. Cache size is measured in megabytes.
9. **Zero-Day Model Update Size**
   The storage required for emergency updates. Size is measured in megabytes.

10. **Zipped Model Archive**
    Compressed AI model files. Archives reduce megabytes required.

NOTES:

NOTES:

NOTES:

NOTES:

NOTES:

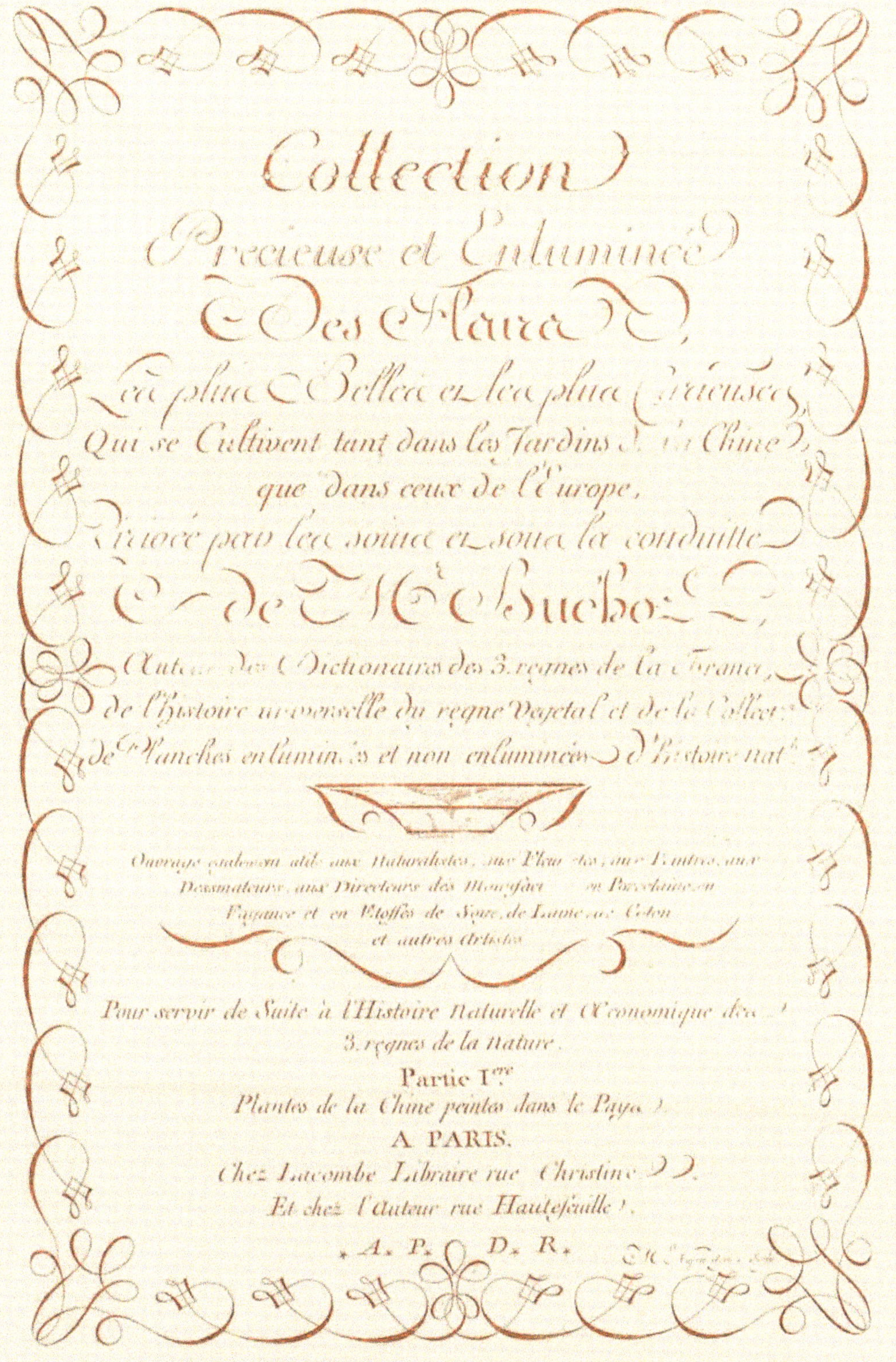

Collection
Precieuse et Enluminée
Des Fleurs
Les plus Belles et les plus Curieuses,
Qui se Cultivent tant dans les Jardins de la Chine
que dans ceux de l'Europe,
Dirigée par les soins et sous la conduitte
de M.r Buc'hoz,
Auteur des Dictionaires des 3. regnes de la France,
de l'Histoire universelle du regne Vegetal et de la Collect.n
des Planches enluminées et non enluminées d'Histoire nat.le

Ouvrage egalement utile aux Naturalistes, aux Fleuristes, aux Peintres, aux
Dessinateurs, aux Directeurs des Manufact. en Porcelaine, en
Fayance et en Etoffes de Soye, de Laine, et Coton
et autres Artistes

Pour servir de Suite à l'Histoire Naturelle et Oeconomique des
3. regnes de la Nature.

Partie I.re

Plantes de la Chine peintes dans le Pays.

A PARIS.

Chez Lacombe Libraire rue Christine.

Et chez l'Auteur rue Hautefeuille.

A. P. D. R.

Pl. 1.

Pl. II

繅絲花

紅梨花

Pl. IV

玉蘭

Pl. V.

牡丹花

Pl. VI.

淡竹花

菊
花

Pl. IX.

辛夷

杜鵑花

卻李花

番山丹花

Pl. 14.

茉莉花

Pl. 15.

山礬花

an malbania?

murraya exotica. Buis de Chine

木
槿

芙蓉

杏花

錦
帶

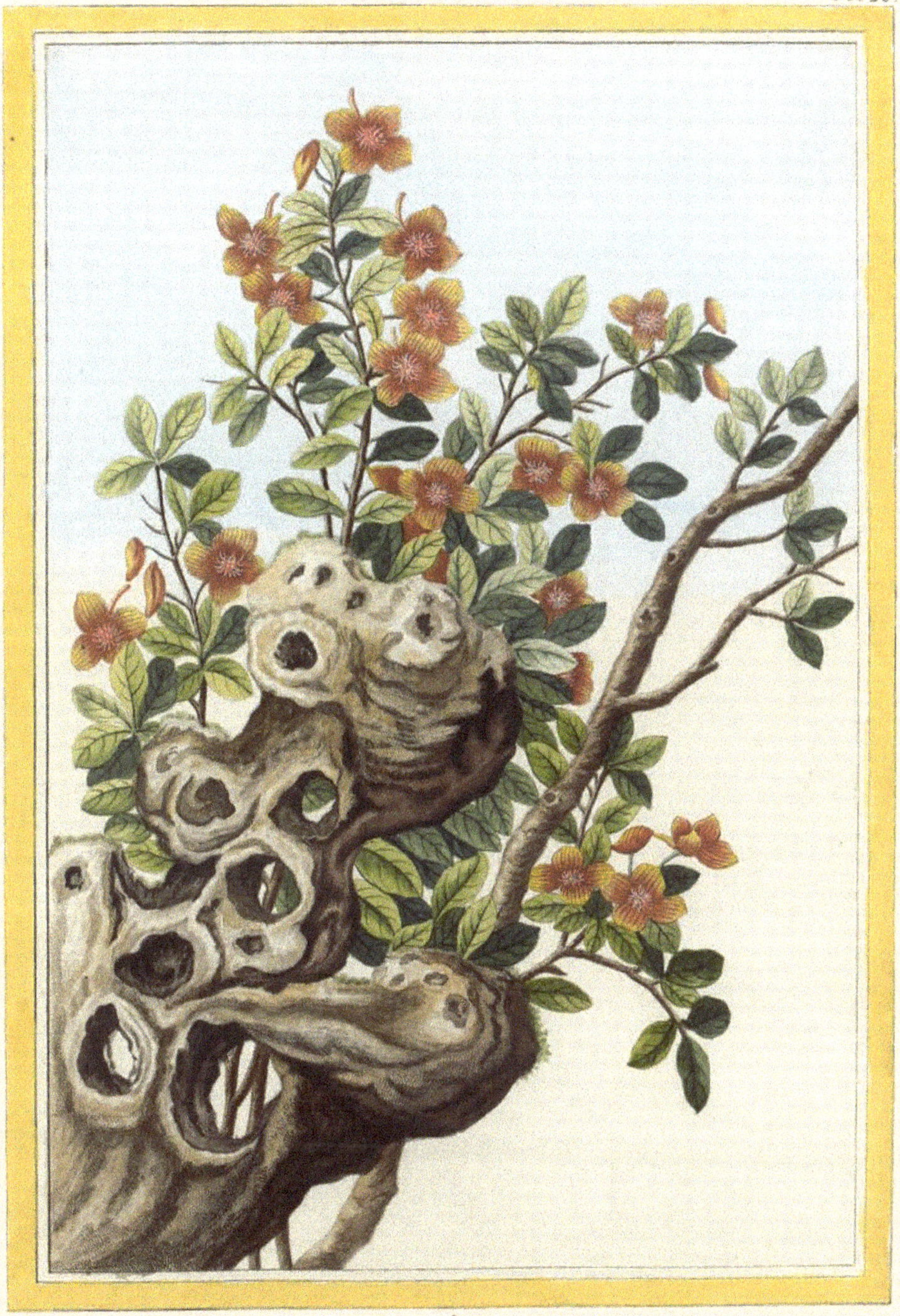

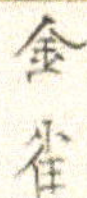
金雀

affinis [illegible].
an Balsamina frutescens?
[illegible] [illegible] Koelreuteria.

Pl. XXI.

玫瑰花

海棠

Pl. XXIII.

Pl.XXIV.

闌天竹

an vitex pinnata. Linn.?

an Commuriam Sinense?

金丝挑

千葉桃

石竹花

Pl. XXVIII.

榴花

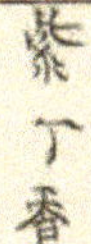
紫
丁
香

夹
竹
桃

Pl. XXXI.

棣棠花

Pl.XXXII.

迎春花

Pl XXXIII.

鷄冠花

Pl.XXXIV.

松
花

Pl. XXXV.

秋海棠

Pl.XXXVI.

郁李花

Pl. XXXVII.

棣棠花

Pl. XXXVIII.

Pl. XXXIX.

Pl. XXXX.

Pl. XII.

荼蘼花

Pl. XLII

Pl XLIII.

Pl. XLIV.

枸杞子

Pl.XLV.

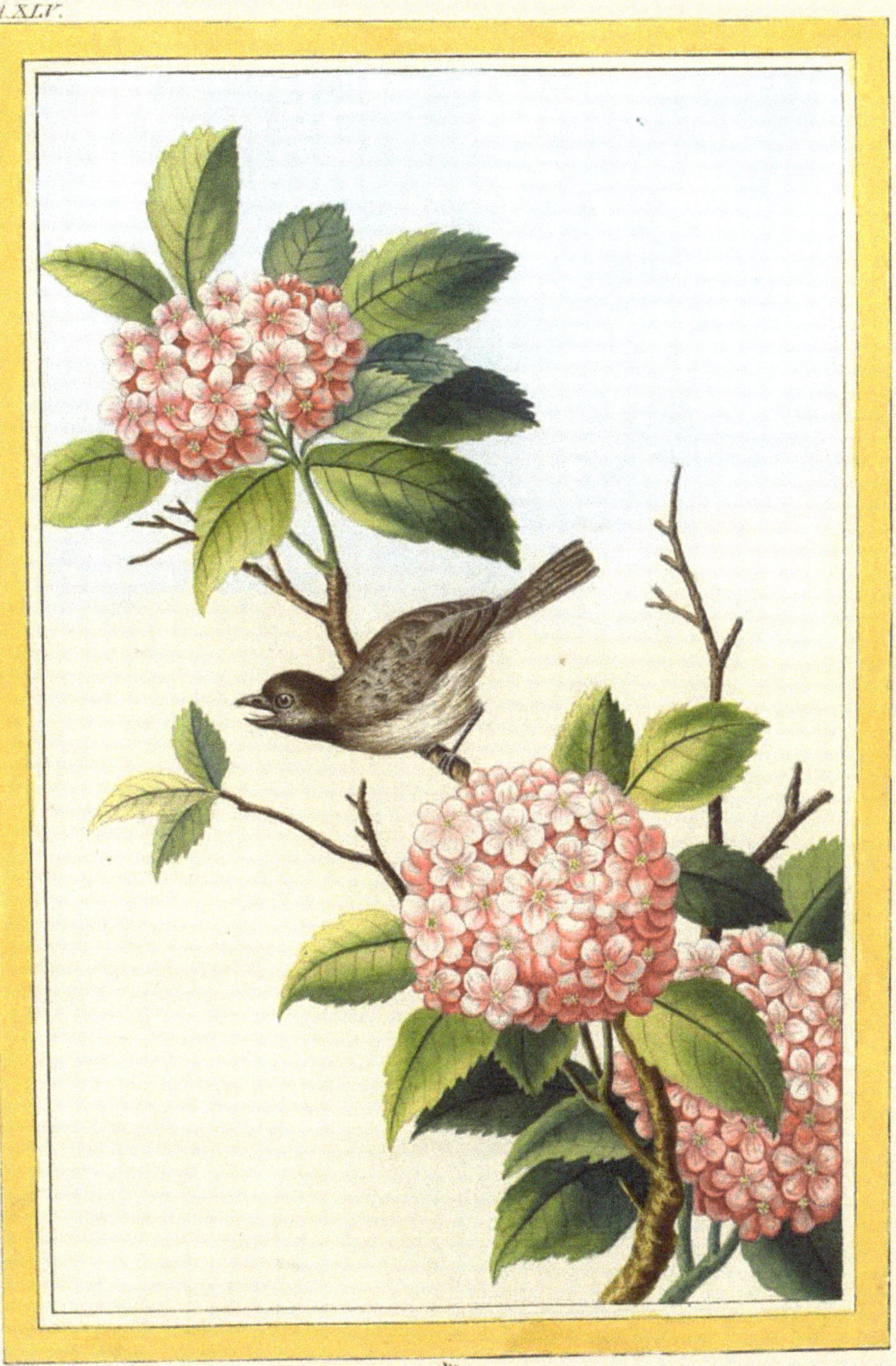

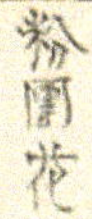

粉團花

primula mutabilis . flos Sinensis
hydrangea. schmidt.
hortensia, Commerson

Pl. XLVI.

海桐花

Pl. XLVII.

萵苣花

Pl. XLVIII.

鐵樹

Pl. XLIX.

単瓣桃

Pl. L.

纏枝牡丹

吉祥草

Pl. 52.

野葡萄

十樣錦

Pl. 64

芍藥花

Pl. 55.

梔子花

凌霄花

紅梅

史君子

Pl. 59.

蠟梅

木香花

Pl. 61.

剪秋羅

金鳳花

平地木

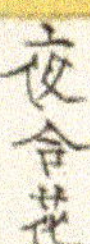

Pl. 65.

美人蕉

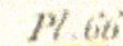
Pl. 66.

玉簪

金銀蓮花

Pl. 68.

錦荔枝

Pl. 70.

靈芝

Pl. LXXI.

Pl. LXXII.

紅[illegible]林花

Pl. LXXIII.

金燈籠

Pl.LXXIV.

蓼花

Pl. LXXV.

Pl. LXXVI.

蕙蘭

Pl. LXXVII.

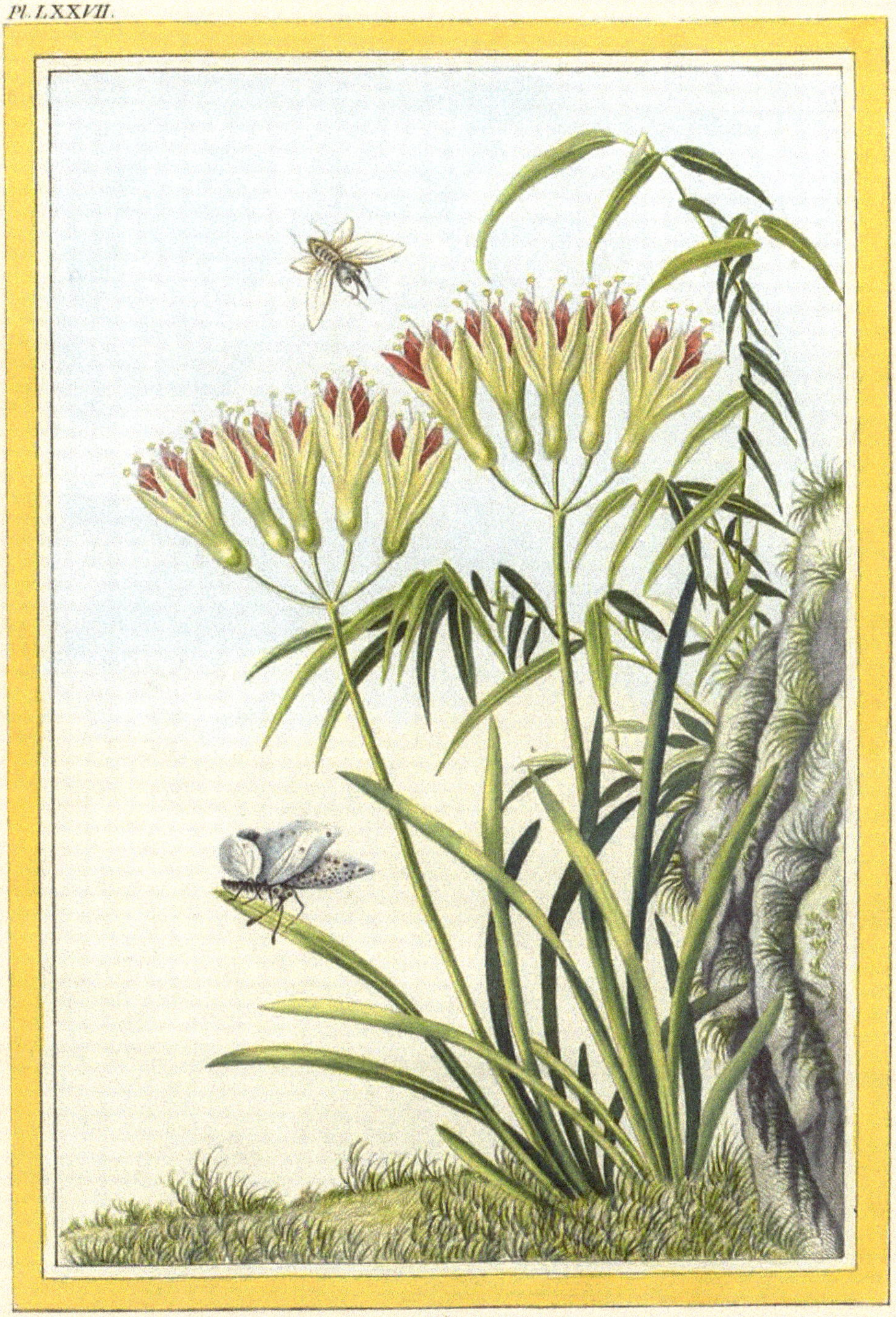

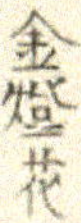

an amaryllis? ou Crinum?

Pl. LXXVIII.

茨菇花

Pl. LXXIX.

蝴蝶花

Pl. LXXX.

番椒

山
茶

Pl. LXXXII.

Pl. LXXXIII.

薔
薇

Pl. LXXXIV

Pl. LXXXV.

白榴花

Pl. LXXXVI

Chrysanthemum indicum, Linn.

Pl.LXXXVII.

地黄根

Pl. LXXXVIII.

Pl. LXXXIX.

木樨

Pl. LXXXX.

Pl.LXXXXI.

Pl.LXXXXII.

Pl.LXXXXIII.

壹捎花

Pl.LXXXXIV.

Pl. LXXXXV.

桃
花

Pl.LXXXXVI.

Pl.LXXXXVII.

荅花

Pl. LXXXVIII.

映山紅

Pl.LXXXXIX.

虎
茨

Pl. C.

Achevé d'imprimer en Angleterre
par Lightning Source UK

www.ingramcontent.com/pod-product-compliance
Ingram Content Group UK Ltd.
Pitfield, Milton Keynes, MK11 3LW, UK
UKHW062008290726
14090UKWH00022B/1462